BLINDMAN'S BLUFF

BLINDMAN'S BLUFF

Richard J. Guzman

Noahs Ark Publishing
Beverly Hills, California

Blindman's Bluff

ISBN 978-0-578-79890-5

Published by:

Noahs Ark Publishing Service
8549 Wilshire Blvd., Suite 1442
Beverly Hills, CA 90211

www.noahsarkpublishing.com

Editor: Geri Keenan
Graphic Design: Christopher C. White
Interior Design: James Sparkman

To my loving wife Frances, you remain my partner in crime and the angel who was always there to carry me through life's challenges! I would not have survived without you by my side.

Contents

INTRODUCTION

In 1995 a favorite colleague of mine, Earl Henry, approached me requesting to write a book about my life. At the time I thought, "Well, this guy wants to write a book about me, I guess I'll do it." Unfortunately, Earl passed away before he could pen my story, and subsequently I shelved the idea for many years. As time progressed, thoughts of writing a book resurfaced, and my reason now is rooted in my mission to educate other blind people facing the same unique challenges that accompany this condition. I want them to move confidently in the world they live in and hopefully my story can help them accomplish this goal.

I rarely use a cane unless I travel out of town to play in my band, to a retreat or some type of special event. A long time ago I was taught how to strengthen and use my senses to walk gingerly and with stealth by a native American Indian friend. When walking I learned to detect rises in sidewalks well before they were approached, so as not to trip. Others in my position need to know they don't have to be so dependent on other people or things. They too can travel within their communities with confidence, fulfill their dreams and goals and survive with pride.

I attended a school for the blind and hated it! It wasn't for me. Four years prior to enrolling in this school, I'd graduated from college. Administration enrolled me in remedial reading, remedial math, and spelling. My spelling book is geared for students in first to eighth grades! Can you imagine how I felt?

The experience was demoralizing. I became angry. The first thing the instructors made me do is sit in a warehouse with other blind people. Everyone was doing the exact same thing, emptying boxes of snap candies. You know...those candy snaps that kids buy as after school treats. We snapped the candies off of these thin strips, put them into large boxes and threw the boxes away. To this day I still have no idea why they had us do that. It was pure nonsense! So, I'm sitting there and after an hour and a half I lost it! I rushed through the job and ran the school out of candy on the first day. On day two the school made me do it all over again. It was maddening!

Being blind does not imply lack of intelligence. It simply means you can't see. That's it! In fact, we may just be a little bit smarter because our additional senses are heightened making our perceptions keener than the average person.

I don't want other young blind students to spend their valuable time on stupid exercises that are meaningless and lack motivation.

Blind or sighted, people should grow to understand they are fully capable of living a normal life. Not only are they capable of living a normal life, they are also able to live it with gusto! Blind people can participate in the world around them, enjoy activities that many experience and find great satisfaction working good jobs in their communities. Their only limitation is their belief system. Blindman's Bluff endeavors to strengthen weak systems.

I was reviled by my family members. My mother didn't like me, my father was abusive and absent, and I was pretty much left to make a life for myself at an early age. In spite of these hardships, and they were unimaginably hard, I overcame them to find purpose and joy.

If I can ascend to find happiness and fulfillment so can others. I married the love of my life, played the trumpet, xylophone and drums in a traveling band and currently teach college courses. Every now and then my band still gigs!

Do you have dreams that you currently believe are impossible to realize because you are blind? If blindness isn't your challenge, what is standing in your way? My life is spread open on these pages. May my fellow blind and sighted comrades, young and old, facing walls that seem impenetrable, find within these pages just what they need to keep moving forward!

CHAPTER ONE
HOME IN THE HOSPITAL

Sixty-nine years ago, at time's divine hand, I was born and targeted into the great city of St. Louis, MO. I rank third in my company of three females and one male sibling. Yes, I am one of two males who grew up in a home filled with passionate Italian women.

Adventuresome. A characteristic bundled with me at birth and resides with me to this day. At age three, my competitive nature was clear to everyone. I remember grabbing some gumption and climbing a sliding board...the wrong way! A sliding board is not a toy. It's a specific type of board usually made of wood, plastic or metal. It is used as a bridge to transfer a person from one surface to another. Kids are genius when it comes to creating toys out of anything and I considered myself a member of that club. Once I watched another kid on my block attempt to use one and I just couldn't wait to try it out. So, there I went! At first it looked pretty easy but after a few seconds into my amateur acrobatic attempt, my foot slipped, I fell, and the retaliatory board fell on my leg and broke my femur bone. Not many people remember things that happened to them at age three, but I tell you what, I will never forget that day! It is forever etched in my mind! I don't remember what happened right after my fall, but I do remember laying on a hospital bed with my leg in a cast raised in the air, higher than the rest of my body. The hospital didn't have it all together back then like they do now. After all, this happened over sixty years ago, and our world had yet to discover its current technological savvy. Life was hard. My little three-year-old body suffered miserably, and I spent almost two weeks on my back in the hospital.

This was my second time as a hospital patient. I was beginning to feel like a regular tenant. There are a series of incidences that landed me back within this medical confine. Spending two whole weeks in what seemed a big, cold building without any friends or family was torture. I wanted to be at home among the things that were familiar to me. Even if those things were unpleasant at times.

We lived on Southwest when I broke my leg on that sliding board and remained there until I was nineteen years old. The residence was a typical two-story brick house with a basement. The Italian custom was to build the kitchen downstairs in the basement which we counted as the first floor. The kitchen and living room were also downstairs on the first floor. The second floor held my parent's bedroom as well as the kids. My three sisters and I slept in the same room and thank goodness we all had our own beds. My maternal great aunt and great-grandmother occupied the two bedrooms on the third floor.

We grew up middle class. My dad worked for La Clede Gas Company, so I'd say we were well provided for. We lived half a block away from Sublette Park on The Hill, a majority Italian community. My sister Rosa, the eldest was age five, Barb was four, I was three, and the youngest, Jeanette was two when I fell. We were stair steps.

Barb, Jeanette and I have a disease named Retinitis Pigmentosa. Both of our parents had the genetics for it. This disease skips the first child. Now, if my mother had skipped one year getting pregnant, Barbara would not have contracted it. But because she had us one right after the other, the second, third and fourth children were hit. Three out of four of us are blind. Rose Marie, who died ten years ago of cancer and Eugene who was born twelve years after me are my only sighted siblings.

My parents were not blind. Once I discovered I would go blind, I asked my uncle, an ophthalmologist, about the disease and he responded with a black and white answer, "I don't know what you're talking about and don't ever ask me again!" Now is that Italian or what? When I didn't get a satisfactory answer from him, I asked my mother, and you know what she said? The same exact thing my uncle said! "I don't know what you're talking about don't ever ask me again!" Yes, you've read that correctly. What did I do? Accepted it like we were taught. We all did.

I had already started wearing glasses at the time. My teachers told my parents it was time for me to buy my first pair, so they took me to my first eye exam. At age five, I was chasing my sister upstairs to the third floor. As I approached the door, she ran through it to hide from me, and slammed it in my face so hard I was knocked down the stairs, causing me to bite off part of my tongue and rip the skin from my chin. I had to get stitches again, so back to the hospital I went.

I was the sickest child amongst my siblings. Every childhood illness discovered me first. I contracted the measles, and the chicken pox between five and eight years old. At eight years old I suffered a heart attack, a by-product from contracting rheumatic fever. One night I woke up screaming and crying in agony at the top of my lungs because my kidneys had begun to fail, and the pain in my back was excruciating. I was rushed to Faith Hospital. The first thing they did was shoot me with penicillin which caused a terrible reaction and made my feet swell three times their normal size. This was my third visit to the hospital and again, I remained there for two weeks. This hospital was beginning to feel like a home away from home.

One evening there was a lot of chaos and ruckus going on in the hospital hallway. Being a nosey little kid, I wanted to see firsthand what was going on. The doctor didn't allow me to get out of bed because I couldn't walk, so I sat on the edge of my bed straining to see what all the commotion was about. That move didn't prove successful, so my next brilliant plan was to bite the inside of my lip on purpose to get the nurse's immediate attention. It worked! I called out to her to let her know my mouth was bleeding. Right away she sped to my beside to survey my injury. Her diagnosis was, I would be just fine. While I had the chance I quickly asked, "So what's going on?" The nurse simply answered, "Nothing." She knew what I was up to. I wasn't fooling anybody. Her name was Mrs. Snyder, and boy was very upset. Not so much with my hospital antics, but because she suspected there might be abuse happening in my home. At the time I believe she was petitioning to have me removed from my parents' care. She was right. My dad was taking a belt to all of us. We would have to lean over the couch as he beat us repeatedly. He found a type of dysfunctional pleasure doing it. Mrs. Snyder had been trying to get me out of the house. I don't know how she found out our father was being abusive toward us. I suppose she intuitively saw the signs. The only visitors I received while I was in the hospital were my parents, just Mom and Dad.

My great-grandmother passed away while I was in the hospital. When I asked what happened, I was told she died from stress. She couldn't speak English, but her Italian was beyond excellent. When we heard the words, "La scopa de gula" aka "I'm going to kick your asses" we would run all the way down the steps of our house.

She was very upset the night I was taken to the hospital and screamed at my parents, Mom and Dad. She was trying to tell them that something was severely wrong with me. She was so worried and upset. That was the last time I saw my Nana. She had a heart attack, and it is believed she was so upset because I was hospitalized. I was the closest grandchild to her. She had a very special place in her heart for me. No one told me she died until I returned home from the hospital and I was heartbroken upon hearing the news.

CHAPTER TWO
MOM HATES RICHARD

My mother never really showed up for me in the way I felt she should. She didn't like me, and as a result told me she didn't and took her hatred for my father out on me. Even in my weakest hours.

A common saying these days is, "Hurt people, hurt people." It is not unusual to find those who have been abused becoming abusers. I don't know much about my mother's past, but I assume she must have been deeply hurt sometime during her formative years. Her father came to the states from Italy in 1908 when he was between eight and ten years old. My mother and her sisters hated him, but we never knew why. Unfortunately, she ended up marrying men she really didn't get along with. Mom was young and had four kids in a row, hated it and felt stuck in life.

Taking care of me while I was ill was an obvious chore. She abhorred the responsibility, but never abandoned me. As strange as this may sound, there is something mildly redeemable about that.

My mother constantly complained about having to carry me from the first floor to the bathroom on the second floor. To get back to my bedroom I would sit down on the steps and go down one step at a time on my own. I tried hard to be self-sufficient to appease her and make things less antagonistic. I never allowed her dislike to create any problems. I accepted her behavior and moved on the best I could. At the same time my dad was abusing me with beatings.

I'm from a neighborhood where you had to be strong with killer like instincts. Even at ten years old you had to think like the mafia. One day I was at the park, got into a fight and beat a kid's butt. His name was Mark, and he was a year or two older than me. My dad taught me how to fight. He took me out to the backyard when I was nine years old and said, "I'm going to teach you how to fight! Put your hands up." So, I put my hands up even with my shoulder. He had me swing at him. I swung at him, he hit me in the jaw, and I went down to the ground. Then he says, "Come on get up and put your hands up." So, I get up, put my hands in the same spot and boom he hits me on the other side of my cheek knocking me down again. I raised up slowly, but this time watching how he protected himself. Now I'm beginning to figure things out. I stood up but backed off from him a little where he couldn't reach me. When he swung this time, I had my hands fixed higher by my jaw, pushed his hand aside and hit him in the chest. He started to laugh. My dad was a Golden Gloves boxer, so he was tickled that I hit him in the chest. Lesson learned? I stayed down on the ground a little longer and assessed the situation before I got up.

Once I went to the barbershop to get a haircut but didn't have it cut short enough for my dad's approval. My Mom was working at Arlean's Department Store part time. When my father saw my hair, he took his belt off and hit me real hard one good time. I immediately saw red, grabbed the belt and we commenced to wrestling. We got so caught up in our match that he ended up standing with his back to my second floor bedroom window and I pushed him right through it while we were both still hanging onto the belt. I looked down to see him hanging there still wrestling with me. Finally, he returned to his senses and stopped struggling while hanging midair. The look on his face was priceless. He was the clear definition of a deer caught in the headlights. The look on his face said, "What in the hell am I doing?" I let go, ran out of my bedroom, out the front door, down the porch, jumped on my bike and took off.

An uncle of mine lived in Bourbon, MO. We used to visit him at least once a month, so I thought I'd ride there. It's ninety miles away and an all two-lane highway on Route 66. Boy, was it hilly. I rode as far as Beaumont and suddenly realized I had no idea how to get to his house once I would arrive. I stopped right in my tracks and turned around. Certainly, I couldn't return to my house, so I decided to ride back to my grandfathers who lived two blocks away from us. My journey started at 3:30 in the afternoon and ended at approximately 8:00 p.m. by the time I got there.

Now, my bike was a one speed, so you know what that means. It was very slow. In addition to that, my sight was declining. During that stage of progression, I could only see twenty feet ahead of me at the most. I wasn't fully aware of the severity of my condition. I truly had no idea. Everything was affected by my poor eyesight. When I read books, my nose would literally almost touch the pages. I would read one line then look for the next one. But my memory was excellent! I retained every word.

When I finally arrived at my grandfather's house, I called my mom at work and she told me to stay there until she got home. I tried taking his phone off the hook just in case my dad called looking for me. I kept hanging the phone up when it rang because a busy signal would sound if I kept it off the hook too long, and I knew he would hear it. I survived until 10:00 p.m. when my mom picked me up. When we got home, he commenced to beating the hell out of me and he hit her too.

Mom and Dad's fighting continued to escalate. Dad's abuse with us kids was intensifying as well. I believe he was sexually abusing my oldest sister Rose and was cheating outside of the home on my Mom.

When my Mother got pregnant again in 1962, she kicked him out of the house. I thought the reason for their divorce was my fault because I got a cheap haircut. That's when I really became a man. In a very blunt, black and white way she straight up told me that from then on, whatever I needed or wanted I'd have to pay for myself. Pants, shoes, whatever. I had to provide for myself, including my private school education. Sounds kind of crazy doesn't it? I was only eleven years old, didn't have a job and still in elementary school. My mother didn't allow me to attend public school. I would have enrolled in Missouri's school system to save money but that was never going to be an option. She told me, "I can't afford you." At eleven years old I went to a private school and paid for it with my cutting grass jobs. She did provide for my sisters though. Well, that's how she grew up. I don't believe she was trying to make a difference between me and my sisters. I didn't look at it as unfair, I took it as life, and this is just the way the world worked in her universe.

LIFE AS A CHILD

My cousin Ralph entered Seminary and I thought I'd follow in his footsteps. These thoughts transpired after I was stricken with rheumatic fever. When standing at death's door one tends to contemplate the spiritual side of their humanity. My sister and I played pretend often and I would stand on the bed and act like a priest mimicking the Latin language they spoke during mass. We were really practicing a full out mass service. That lasted all of two weeks and I let go of the lofty idea. My cousin Ralph also quit shortly thereafter. What a short-lived dream some would say, but we were kids and that's just how we moved through life. I used to visit Ralph's house because his younger brother had a drum set. Every time we visited his home, I rushed to play his drums, and just banged away. He was a year older than me and took drum lessons.

I didn't really have any ambition before I was ten years old and had no idea what I wanted to do. After my great-grandmother died, we remodeled the upstairs where she and my aunt lived. My sisters couldn't wait to move up to the top floor. When they moved upstairs, I got the whole bedroom to myself. I started drawing and got to be pretty good at it too. In my eighth grade year my teacher gave me a page of cars and asked me to draw them all. There were twenty-five cars on that page, and I drew about ten of them, and she kept them. Not too shabby. In eighth grade I really became interested in music. In grades prior to that I was into protecting my buddies, starting fights playing football or whatever the sport was for the season.

MUSIC – THE ESCAPE

In 1962 my Uncle Warren was drafted. Before he left, he gave me his trumpet and my love for music and musicianship began. I had been beating on paint cans for years with paint brushes and pencils. The true mark of a drummer in the making.

I began trying to teach myself musical notes and how to read music and did pretty well if I do say so myself. My dad was the Boy Scout leader in our parish, but I decided to join the troupe after he quit. I became the club bugler. The type of music I was interested in playing were songs like The Taste of Honey by the Tijuana Brass. My friend Bill Moreland decided we were going to create a band. I had a snare drum, a symbol, disassembled a music stand and made a cymbal stand. At the ripe age of twelve we started playing and became really good. Our name started to spread across the area and churches started hiring us to play at various functions. During a first break at one event a bunch of teenage girls came up to the stage and asked where the rest of my drums were. My ego stood up and lied to make me look good. I told them someone broke into the house and stole them. They didn't stop there and continued by asking, "So why didn't they take this?" I told them there wasn't a case, so they let it go. I was quick with the come backs. The stage we played on was hollow so when I stomped my foot it sounded like a bass drum. No one knew the difference.

When I turned fourteen my mother said she would co-sign a drum set for me, but it would be my responsibility to pay it off. I didn't waste any time and purchased a drum set from Danaher's Music store. I paid them off by cutting lawns, washing windows, doing odd jobs for people and cleaning cars. My fee was a dollar fifty per lawn. My drums cost four hundred dollars. I put one hundred bucks down and the rest is history.

Surely the questions have rolled through your mind, "Well if your mother hated you so much why did she help you buy the drums?" My answer is, I'm not altogether certain. I was her son and I believe deep down inside she knew her problems were not my fault. I hadn't asked to be brought into this world. She knew it was unfair, but I believe she did the best she could with what she had be it miniscule.

CHAPTER THREE
LEARNING TO WALK

After fighting rheumatic fever, I had to learn how to walk again. My doctors warned me against walking for six months as doing so would put too much stress on my heart. When six months ended, I began to work on strengthening my legs. The only thing I could do was try to stand up. I had an allergic reaction to penicillin when I was in the hospital and my feet had swollen big as balloons. The doctors took me off the penicillin and prescribed another antibiotic to counteract its effects. I needed so much help and attention that Mrs. Snyder became involved in my healing process. She sensed I was not being properly taken care of at home and detected the truth about my relationship with my mother. Mrs. Snyder was a saint to take me on as a personal responsibility.

Learning to walk again was challenging to say the least. I created my own physical therapy routines to help me grow stronger. At first, I would stand in front of the couch in the basement for a few moments. That little bit of exertion made my legs grow weary so I'd sit down. Giving up wasn't an option so I would try again a little later. My mother and father couldn't be relied upon for help as mom was too busy with everything else and dad wasn't around. At this point I was her problem and constant nag, yet I still needed her help. I gained weight and got fat because I couldn't move around. There wasn't enough room in the basement for me to move around in my wheelchair but I finally got the bright idea to use it as an aid for walking. The wheelchair became my cane! The more I walked the stronger my legs got. Soon I was able to go in the backyard. There were forty or fifty kids on our block, and I'd watch them all play in their backyards. I would sit or stand and watch them all playing ball, jumping rope, playing dodge ball and all the other games kids enjoy. I was eight years old and wished to play but still wasn't strong enough. What I could do was turn a jump rope, and little by little my strength returned. Finally, I was able to maneuver more comfortably and became aggressive at making myself better because no one else was going to do that for me.

Eventually, Mrs. Snyder became a second thought. My immaturity didn't allow me to fully understand the benefit she provided. Before I was able to walk, I had to start making my way up to the second floor to use the bathroom. Sitting on the steps and moving up one step at a time was my mode of transportation. My mother said carrying me up the stairs was too hard for her. So, I made my way to the stairway in my wheelchair and sat my way up each step, one at a time. When I got to the top of the stairs I would stand up and hold on to the walls to guide me where I needed to go. The bathroom was right around the corner at the top of the stairs so thankfully it wasn't far away. When leaving the bathroom to go back downstairs I'd scooch myself down each step.

The archbishop from our neighborhood parish heard of my malady. He never visited the parishioners' homes, but he made an exception one time and that's when he came to my house at the beginning of April to confirm me. Boy, did his visit make me feel special. Though church was only one block from the house, it was too far away for me in my condition.

Getting along with the neighborhood kids was my primary goal so little by little I was able to accomplish more. Moving the coffee table and walking the length of the couch and around the room to the back of the kitchen was one of my unique regimens. Finally, my strength returned, and I was able to walk around and hang out with neighborhood friends. That's how I did it. I hung out with the neighbors and my sisters until I was strong enough to play certain games but with limitations. By the end of summer, I was back to walking and running and it felt good. The final feat to accomplish was riding my bike. When I turned nine in June, I was finally able to ride. So, I rode my bike and built my endurance.

Herb was the name of a man who would hang out at the park everyday no matter what season of the year. No one knew his last name but what everyone did know is that he played for the Cardinals. He lived one block away from my house and always asked me to come over to his. One day I finally did. The first thing he did was pull out the Holy Bible and start talking about the different stories, Jesus, salvation and tried to interest me in reading it. Honestly, back then I could really care less. At that age, I was only interested in hanging out with the kids on my block and playing sports.

Herb also began sharing that he was part Indian and showed me a unique way of walking. Now my curiosity was peaked. I was very interested to learn as much as I could. He could walk on a pile of leaves and hardly make a sound, starting with the heel of the foot then gently rolling downward to the balls of the feet. Walking heel to toe with my poor eyesight helped me not trip and fall and I became more confident walking on my own. This method Herb taught me helps guard against what's coming and to anticipate.

After he showed me the steps, I would practice on my own. At eleven and twelve years old I thought it was so cool and didn't realize until I got older, how much this skill would be of help to me. Herb also taught me how to walk on the sides of my feet and heels. He told me that when Indians walked through the forest, they sometimes could not see what was on the ground. If you made too much noise, you might get killed.

No one was certain of Herb's age. My mother and other people warned me to be careful of him as he could have been a pedophile. We only worked together for a month. After that, I still saw him at the park everyday ready to play ball with whoever showed up.

CHAPTER FOUR
The Terrible Years

My terrible years started in 1962 when I was eleven years old and ended when I was nineteen. When the new school year began, I got a job! My Uncle Jess had a friend named Harriet who was instrumental in helping me get hired at a Hunter's Concession Stand. We worked Washington University, Ritenour High School, Normandy High School and a few other places. The owner of the company also owned a Mister Softee truck. The job was fun because of our job atmosphere but we worked hard carrying and unloading ice, selling concessions, stocking and selling merchandise and even working as security.

I worked all the games, basketball, football and wrestling. At Thanksgiving we worked Washington University's Thanksgiving Day game. A day's work was always unpredictable. You never knew what might happen. Once I was helping a customer and out of nowhere, a guy jumped over the counter, grabbed all the money and started running. Immediately I ran out the back door and chased him throughout Washington University's campus starting at Francis Field, then down the side street, past the big hall and into the parking lot. When I finally caught up with him, we both went down. I tackled him! A guard had followed me and noticed I hadn't seen the guy I was chasing throw his knife away in the parking lot. When I tackled him my pants ripped, and my knee rammed hard into the ground. The guard grabbed him, returned him to the crime scene and made him empty his pockets. We were lucky and got most of the money back. I was only twelve years old and the thief was probably seventeen to nineteen years old. I could run, I was fast, and I was absolutely fearless!

A surprise came to our family when I was twelve years old. My baby brother Eugene Guzman was born in the Spring of 1963. He grew up not knowing his father at all. Bill had left my mom that same year right before Christmas. Gene was spoiled rotten by all of us although my sisters had more influence over him than I did. We did the things big brothers and little brothers do together. I took him to hockey games when he was about five years old and would sit him high on my shoulders so he could see everything. My sisters were always competing with me for his attention and didn't like me taking him places so I didn't get to take him out that much. In 1975, he turned twelve years old and decided he wanted to follow in my footsteps. I'd say he's done well as he is one of the baddest drummers here in St. Louis. It's funny looking back on old conversations. I remember sitting around with Gene and Mike as they recounted a story about their youthful pride and ignorance. They told me they were complaining about having to learn "dumb" songs from the fifties and sixties. Lo' and behold, one year later Eugene is gigging with Chuck Berry and getting paid seven hundred fifty dollars for one hour's worth of playing. We laugh about it now.

I went from being a good kid to fronting as a hoodlum. I was mad at the world because in my mind, I had broken up our family. Fighting became my coping mechanism. I protected many of my friends when they were harassed or being picked on. If someone tried to pick a fight with my buddies, I would jump in between them and the other guy and scare him off. No one intimidated me and no one messed with me either.

Achieving good grades in school was a no brainer. I made good grades. Some nuns were strict, and others were kind and patient There was one nun I really liked. A guy had written a bunch of things about her on little sheet of paper that somehow got circulated to a broad audience. I got blamed for being that kid because everybody's penmanship looked like mine. I had three or four clients that I did homework for who were doing well in math. I was an entrepreneur at heart and didn't even know it. For two years I was busy making business sales and did everybody's math homework for five cents per sheet. That was big money back then.

We were all in the eighth grade. The principal of the school who was also an eighth grade teacher called me out into the hallway and said, "Why did you write that note." I said, "I didn't write it." She smacked me across the face and said, "Quit lying to me!" Her favorite saying was, "If you lie, you'll cheat. If you cheat, you'll steal." She asked again, "Now tell me why you did it." I said, "I didn't do it Sister." Then she hauls off and slaps me across the cheek again. She continues with a harsh command, "You wrote this now own up to it!" I said, "I didn't do it!" Then she tells me, "You're suspended!" So, I go back in the room and Tom Tissi, the guy who wrote the note, tells me, "Don't kill me!" and gives me a dollar fifty. The whole class is listening to all of this and looking at me with questions written all over their faces wanting to know if I was going to really keep silent or fight him. I said, "I'll see you at the park after school." The park is where everything happens. So, he begs me, "Please don't! My braces are new. I will give you anything you want!" He sent me a couple of dollars and begged me not to kick his butt. After school he comes up to the park and gives me another five bucks. This went on for two days. In the meantime, this friend of mine named Salvatore decides he's going to defend Tom. The next morning, I catch Salvatore on the way to school and beat him up. I got him before he could get me. At lunch time, on his way home, I kicked his butt again. Later on, in school he apologized and said he shouldn't have interfered and was sorry. Well, on the way home from school I caught him again and just made sure he would never do it again. He tried to fight back but gave up. It was no use.

I was always fighting. I'd go to the park and get in a fight on purpose. If we were playing ball and somebody cheated, an argument would heat up and the next thing you know a fight was on and I was all about it. We lived on The Hill. There was a certain prestige one had living on those neighborhood streets. We couldn't lose. You could say we were trying to fight our way into the Italian code to become a Goomba.

In my seventh and eighth grade years I was very competitive with the other students. I still worked the concession stands and made good money. I was able to contribute one hundred dollars for lent. During lent you sacrifice something. I wanted to give up my anger, but it just wouldn't allow me to let go.

In eighth grade I broke some guy's shoulder. We were playing football and he was on the opposing team. He was a ninth grader. I hit him just right and he went home hurt that day. I had developed a protector reputation image.

Things were going well, and I was trying to prove I was King of the Hill but there was one guy in my way, Dave Palmisano. During the summer between seventh and eighth grade he kicked my butt one good time, and I wasn't going to let it happen again. So, one day we were in the gym and I purposed to make him so mad he couldn't see straight. One of the best strategies to engage during a fight is to make your opponent mad to where they can't focus. That's how I was taught. You talk so much smack at them and get them so mad they become unfocused then you go in for the kill. It's all mental. In order to have a good fight you must be clear minded combined with great mental acuity. Dave Palmisano was slap happy and I was able to knock the tar out of him before anyone could break us up. Bill taught me that. He knew all the tactics and strategies on how to win. Professional fighters know the art of intimidation before they encounter the actual fight. They get in their opponent's head and most of the time, it works. Bill taught me well.

My Summer at Otties'

During the summer between my eighth and ninth grade year I worked as a short order cook at Ottie's Southwest Pizza located about a block and a half from my house. Work for me began at around three thirty p.m. and I'd start each day by shaping the pizza dough, making sure it was nice and fluffy.

My grandfather Jesse would stop by sometimes and help himself to some anchovies right out of the bin. I'd never tasted anchovies and decided to try them. Why in the world did I do that? They tasted horrible! I opened the door and spit it all outside.

So, I'm fourteen years old working at Otties and there's a basement in the restaurant where all the booze and wine were kept. I discovered a grate right in front of the building that led right down into that basement. One day my friends, Bill and Warren came by and we snuck down there. Once inside, I scrounged around, found a paper bag and put two bottles of Mogen David in it. I handed Bill one of the bottles and we both started drinking. We ended up not liking the wine so much but what the heck, it was free. I worked six days a week, only taking one day off the whole time I worked there. Later that summer I'm hanging out at the park with my friends and see my boss coming toward me. She came up to the park to take me back to work. Talk about awkward. She owned Otties. I had called in sick, but she didn't believe me. She came to my house which is a little over a block away from the restaurant. We always left the front door open and she came inside and saw no one was home. When she found me at the park, she walked right up to my face and like a sergeant shouted the order, "You're going to work, you're not sick!" What could I do? I went home, changed my attire and went to work. I was so fed up that I had to work. I was fourteen years old working while everyone else was out having a good time. But this one lesson taught me a good work ethic — hard work and perseverance. I was paying for everything myself. High school was coming up and I needed money.

Fights were a dime a dozen. My buddies, Bill Moreland and his brother had their bikes stolen. I found out the thief was a guy who lived eight blocks away. His name was Joe Calcaterra. So, I go to his place with Bill. Joe was decidedly bigger than us and he had this white German Shepherd. As I approached his gate, he started to sic his dog on me. I warned him if he opened that gate and his dog came out, I would kill it. He told me I couldn't, and I told him he didn't want to find out. I was known for my mean reputation, so he put the dog inside his house. Even though Joe was three inches taller than me, I walked up to him and said, "I'm here to get Bill's bike back and if you don't give it us, I'm going to beat the s*** out of you." From that moment on, we were friends and hung out all the time.

During my freshman year I played on the football team. One day I was standing around talking to a bunch of the guys in a space where we couldn't be seen. A bunch of them were smokers and pulled out their cigarettes. I had my back to a window and the principal was in another building across the way looking down at us through her second-floor window. The day was cold and my breath formed a mist as I was talking and breathing so she thought I was smoking with the guys too. I wasn't smoking at all. She took it upon herself to call my mother and suspended me along with everyone else for three days as well as slap me on the cheek again! That seemed to be her favorite thing to do.

BAD BOY ANTICS

Things can get boring for kids with short attention spans. Some of us probably really did have attention deficit disorder and didn't know it. We were just plain old undisciplined and extremely mischievous or super smart. One day, Pat Hamilton and two other guys took the hinges off one of the bathroom doors that opened outward into the school hallway. When they knew the assistant principal was going to be on that end of the building, they lit a cherry bomb and flushed it down the toilet. Of course, it blew the heck out of the toilet. The assistant principal comes running through the door and it falls on the culprits! All the kids come running out of the bathroom, stepping all over the door and running over the assistant principal. Pat and I were pulled into the office and really got the third degree burned into us because the assistant principal's suit was ruined! We were laughing like crazy and could barely talk because it was so funny. The principal was interrogating us and we laughed right in her face. All of this was happening at around noon and we still had three hours to go before school let out. Every hour, for the rest of the day, she pulled us out of our classrooms, split us up and tried to get us to rat each other out. It didn't work and we held on to our awesome secret!

I was in and out of trouble at school because I hung with people who smoked and attempted silly stunts. After the incident with the bathroom door, the school was only interested in getting rid of us. The tuition was a thousand bucks per year, and I was responsible for paying it all. At the end of the school year I was about three or four hundred dollars short so it was recommended that I switch schools because I wouldn't be able to pay it off. I would have gladly gone to public school but already knowing my mother's stance, wouldn't beg her. She was firm about me going to private schools only. I can't tell you why she wouldn't let me go she just said, "You're not going and that's it!" In 1967, I transferred from Bishop DuBourg High School to a school I didn't want to attend because my sisters Barbara and Jeanette went there, and I didn't want to follow them. I wanted my independence. I really wanted to go to McBride High School, but my score was ten points shy from passing. Saint Francis DeSales High School had three tracts, A, B and C. The A Tract was geared toward very smart or gifted students, B Tract was for students who were average scholastically and the C Tract was for academically challenged students. I was accepted on the B Tract.

I recall that I could not see well enough to even open my locker. The numbers were difficult to read so I left it open all the time. I was in the tenth grade and still wasn't cognizant why my eyes operated this way.

That summer I turned sixteen and my mother gave me a difficult choice to make. She said, "You can have a car or your drums, you can't have them both." What a dreadful choice for a teenager to make, but I made it! Yes, indeed! I sold my drums to my neighbor Ricky Bertoni who lived two doors up from us. After selling my drums, I bought a '61 Ford Fairlane with a three hundred fifty-three engine. That baby moved fast with its powerful V8 engine. I loved it! Of course, I felt cool driving that Fairlane around town. Come on now, here I am in my teenage prime with a car that made me look like a young movie star. All I can say is my ego was pumped!

Shortly thereafter I started working at Clark Oil on Hampton and Westpark, sixteen years old and still unaware I was visually challenged. One would think I'd have finally figured it out. It even puzzles me when I think about it.

Back then attendants pumped gas, checked water levels and washed windows. Once I could not find where to return the dip stick in one of the cars I was attending. Not wanting to appear foolish, I placed the stick under the hood in a place where it wouldn't fall out. Only God knows what happened to the car later that day. It could've caught fire!

One day in my sophomore year I was in biology class with my experiment partner, Stanley Newly, working on a project when he started goofing around. This activity struck the attention of a nun who marched over to our table to inform us we both flunked. There aren't adequate words to express how mad I was, but I found a way to tell Stanley I was going to kick his ass. As soon as the bell rang, I ran out of the classroom and quickly turned around to face the door. When Stanley walked out, I punched him right in the mouth, knocking him back five feet. Two girls caught him before he hit the ground Two days later he came back to school and thought he would show me the same gratitude. In gym class he started a fight with me and in my usual fashion I beat the tar out of him before the coach came over to break us up. The coach broke us up but didn't turn us into the office

It was strange because someone informed him why the fight occurred. He justified it and told us to not let it happen again.

In my junior year I took a typewriting class. The teacher seemed to enjoy picking on me and assigned me as the repair person for all the class typewriters. What? Well, there were girls in class who could type sixty to seventy words per minute. I decided I would repair this one girls ribbon for her. I placed a roll of caps in front of the ribbon. Caps are those little things that pop when ignited leaving a mild gun powder smell in its wake. As soon as this girl started typing the ribbon blows up and right away the teacher says, "Rich you are in trouble!" This nun was old and always gave timeouts. We stole her timer, and all kinds of things. One day I decide it's smoke bomb time. Outside of her window is the roof to the building extension. I got the smoke bomb and rolled it to the back of the room and everybody's screaming, "Fire, fire, fire!" Windows were opened and smoke is everywhere. Everyone was jumping out onto the roof and running out. She locked the door and said, "Nobody's leaving!" Well, I had to scrub the floor. I did all these things knowing I would get in trouble, but I did not care. So, what if I must scrub the floor. I will scrub the floor. Like I said, I had no fear.

No One To Guide Me

There was no guidance in my home. If I wasn't working, I was at school or at the park. I did whatever I wanted to do. My mom gave me a curfew to be inside by midnight. If I missed the bus I would have to walk home, and it was an eight-mile walk. One night I was eight or nine miles away and walking home. I almost tripped over some guy laying on the ground that someone had beaten up. He was down there moaning and groaning so I took off running. A couple of policemen saw me running, stopped me and accused me of beating this guy up and taking his money. Thankfully, they realized it was dark and I couldn't see worth a can of beans. They didn't bring attention to that fact but instead said, "Okay we realize you didn't do it." They asked me what happened, and I said, "That guy was down there moaning and groaning, and I took off running." I still had at least five miles or more to go. Thank goodness I was in good physical shape.

Father Donald Gladsteter was a priest at De Sales. He would take a bunch of us guys out on weekends to make sure we didn't get in trouble. We were juniors and seniors, and he would take us out drinking. My Mom had no idea and of course dad wasn't around.

Father Gladsteter was also the soccer and wrestling coach. I joined the soccer team and did well. In my senior year while we were playing, I jumped up in the air to head a ball. We were playing Chamanade High School. As I and an opposing team player came down, he stuck his knee out and cracked three of my ribs. I could hardly breathe as I tried gasping for air. Father Donald Gladsteter said, "Aww quit faking." I said, "No, no pull me out. I can stand on the sidelines." Three or four weeks pass and we're in playoffs. We went into double overtime and the game was called because it was dark, but I played the best game ever and got two college scholarships out of it. Two days later we played the same team, but I couldn't participate because my ribs were hurting so bad from all that happened the previous game. I just couldn't do it.

It took me six weeks to finally get over my painful rib injury, but believe it or not, I did something even dumber. In 1970, my senior year, the state wrestling championship was on the line. I had never beaten this one guy, Rick Huemueller. He was a good kid and student and had an older brother who died jumping trains. We were both in first place. I went out to the mat to wrestle him and, within five seconds, he falls on my chest and I scream out so loud. The coach throws in the towel and starts cussing and yelling at me, "What are you doing out here wrestling?" I kind of smiled at him and said, "I had to do it." He said I could have forfeited, but I told him I had to give it a try. He asked me if I was trying to kill myself. He yelled at me in front of the entire crowd and he was loud!

We were always pulling stunts. One day my buddy Denny and I

went to North St. Louis to buy some beer. We always went there to buy our alcohol. Our practice was, I would go inside and Denny would wait for me in the car. One night Mike Cissi hangs with us and he is driving. There's five of us in the car. As usual, I go into the store, buy two cases of beer and walk out to the car holding one case in one hand and opening the door with the other. North St. Louis is a tough part of town. We were in one of the roughest areas located on Grand and Cass. As I walked out the store some guys started following me asking for the beer and threatened to take it from me if I didn't. I'm like, "No, get out of here!" Right after those words spill from my mouth I look around and my friends were nowhere in sight. They had split! I'm left standing there wondering where they'd gone. I start walking to the curb and finally they pull up and say, "Hurry up get in, hurry up get in." We barely got away before anything bad happened.

There was another incident where Father Gladsteter took us to Chuck A Burger right outside the city limits. We were all enjoying a nice dinner and I happened to glance at these two beer steins. They were tall solid glass steins. One of the guys dared me to steal one but I had to figure out how to get it out of the restaurant without being noticed. I got it! I'll just carry it in my jacket and sit in the back seat. Nobody knew I had it and I still have it to this day. I was the proverbial Dennis The Menace type.

We did a lot of things in our senior year. With our bold and arrogant selves, Francis, Mike, Joe and I went to a cop bar on 39th and Park in St. Louis. Francis' uncle was tending bar. We sat down at the bar like we were old enough and started drinking with these police officers. They came over to our table and bumped into us like, "What are you doing here?" We sat there as loud as could be, had three beers each, then left. Those were different days. We had some pretty interesting and adventurous growing up years!

Before I graduated in 1970, I was working at Clark Oil on the corner of West Park and Hampton. Joe Calcaterra and Tom Savio were

good friends of mine back then and were making plans to rob me at the station. They said they would come and steal some cigarettes. I told them no, but Joey was determined to do it anyway. Located in the back of Clark Oil was storage space. Joey and Tom jumped the fence making a bunch of noise. When I walked to the back to look around, they ran and took a bunch of cigarettes with them. When the police arrived, I told them I knew who did it and remained at the station until 3:00 a.m. Joe found the courage, came back and returned everything before the police got hold of him. At the time I forgot he was connected to the police. His Dad was a cop!

About five years ago Joe owned a bar called Seven Steps. He was a gambler and had gotten too far in debt. One night his car was found on the middle of the Mississippi River with the doors open and no Joe to be found. He was probably dead before he touched water. Joe was never heard from again, and his wife could not collect the insurance for seven years. The sad part was that he had three kids.

My mother didn't work with me at all. We barely talked. I would have to use the pay phone at the drugstore if I wanted to talk to my girlfriends or anyone else. My sisters hogged the phone and we only had one line. Cell phones weren't even a thought back then. People like to know how I dealt with the treatment from my family, wondering if I walked around in pain because. It hurt but I learned how to deal with it. A lot of my anger grew from the pain of rejection I had pent up inside for so long.

My soul grew up quick. I had to get serious early in life because of my mother's total rejection, my father leaving us and being made to take care of myself, by myself. I fought all the time because I was angry on the inside and that was a way of life for me to work through it as a kid. I wanted to fight, I needed to fight. That was my dysfunctional therapy. I got things out of my system by fighting. I do regret having hurt so many people. In my own immature way fighting was how I navigated and survived through life.

The "Terrible Years" were fighting years seared with recklessness. I was angry and bearing the burden of breaking up my home and the non-relationship with my mother.

Maybe things would have been different if I'd had a father, a real father, who was passionate about raising emotionally healthy kids. Parental guidance is the support every child needs. Though they may shun discipline, there is something settling and comforting knowing someone cares enough to tough love you through life. Kids may not admit it when they are young, but nine times out of ten will appreciate it in the long run.

CHAPTER FIVE
I SHOULD BE DEAD

I shouldn't have lived past fourteen years old. When I was twelve years old, Highway 44 was under construction. Right at Hampton and Wilson the workers created a great big pile of dirt underneath Highway 44. Behind this dirt pile were clay mines and a lot of old torn down buildings. My friends David, Jim and I would go there all the time and fool around making forts and doing all kinds of things boys like to get into. This was our way of having fun away from home. Not all the buildings were torn down though. We ran across the roofs of some that were left standing. One day we were doing our usual running and jumping across roofs. I don't know why but this one particular time I got a late start and was lagging behind the guys. The next thing you know, the third guy to my left fell through the roof and was killed. Scared out of our minds, we stopped, turned around and tried to retrace our steps. We finally got off the roof and got out of there.

We notified the police and told them everything that happened. We were not held responsible for the accident. That's why I said I shouldn't have lived past fourteen. If I had started out before the fella that died, I would've been the one to fall through the roof of that building.

There was a movie theater called the Columbia. The guys and our girlfriends would hang out there and have a good time. None of us were thinking about sex back then. We all just loved to hang out. Because of my bad reputation for fighting, guys liked to test me. One day some guy said he was going to kick my butt. I told Diane, a girl I was with at the time, I'd be right back. One of my friends left ahead of me for the bathroom. I was two or three minutes behind him. Once I got there I could not open the door because they were already up against it fighting! Before you know it, the ushers show up and push me out of the way. They barge in to break up the fight and throw two guys out. While all of this was happening, I ran back to my seat to tell Diane I would be outside. Here again, I'm a couple of minutes behind the program and my friend goes outside and a guy stabs him with an ice pick and kills him. That moment was meant for me. By the time I made it outside he was on the ground dead that quick. I take off running around the corner from the movie theater to my friend Geraldine Seruni's house. I joined her on the porch and watched all of these cops, ambulances and everybody pull up. People standing in the crowd were saying, "That's Rich" because I was the one who was supposed to have had the fight. A blanket was placed over the poor guy that died. I'm sitting on Geraldine's porch not knowing all of this was happening. When things calmed down, I got up and though I was just two blocks away from home, decided to head to the juice store. That's what we called it back then. I go buy a soda and a cupcake, walk out and sit on the steps nervous as can be and still unaware of all the goings on. This cop who had three gorgeous daughters pulls up, gets out of his car, starts hollering at me and slaps me. He said, "You're supposed to be dead! I'm going to take you home. Your mom is having a fit! She thinks you are dead!" I'm like oh my gosh! The man takes me home and brings me in the house. What did my mom do right away? She slapped me right across the cheek and screamed out, "What are you doing here?" The police knew who killed the guy so I'm pretty sure he was put behind bars. Juvenile Hall was his destination, and he was entered into the system for murder. This guy was looking for me because of my reputation. He was a bully with me and my family.

One summer while I was fourteen, my friends and I had gotten our hands on some pink slips that showed us being sixteen. I don't recall how we forged them, but we were all able to go to this motorcycle shop and rent them for fifteen dollars a day. Here we were, fourteen years old and riding motorcycles. I think they were the smallest bikes you could rent. Once a week you'd find us having the time of our lives on these bikes. One day we decide we're going to ride our bikes up that mountain of dirt by Highway 44. Things were going well, we're having a good time coming down that hill when my handlebars become dislodged. I jumped off the bike and everything shut off. It's a heck of a terrain going downhill. So, I jumped off the bike and decided to walk it back down to keep from killing myself. In the meantime, it started raining and the bike starts sliding on the wet pavement. That was no fun, so I returned it to the rental place and got a rain check.

When I was twelve years old my grandfather got me a job as a custodian at the Grand Candy Tobacco Store. This place was a warehouse on Natural Bridge. I took two buses and walked a couple of blocks to get there. It was in North St. Louis which was a bad part of town. I would often take the bus or hitchhike if necessary. The owner would let me in and then leave. This was a candy and cigarette place so I would eat candy while I cleaned. Smoking wasn't my thing but thought hey, why not just take a pack. I made a bad choice, picked up one pack and put it in my coat pocket. It didn't occur to me that cameras were in the place so I was busted. The owner wasn't worried about the candy bars, he wanted to know why I wanted cigarettes. He was pretty kind and gave me a break. I worked another two or three weeks and got tired of getting up early on Saturday mornings. Traveling there was becoming more dangerous. I was getting honked at and people would yell at me out of their windows plus it was getting cold. I would have to go through the hoods and either walk or hitchhike so that was it for me going to Grant Tobacco and Candy Company. I was a working boy with bills to pay. I had to be responsible for a long time and keep myself in blue jeans or Levi's. I bought all of my clothes and needed money, so I had to take certain risks at times.

CHAPTER SIX
PARTY TIME

It all started in 1970 when me and Michael Cissi tried to enlist in the navy during the Viet Nam era. I was working at a drafting company as a shipping clerk and found myself quickly promoting within the company. Turmoil was heating up at home because my stepfather married my mom and she and I were having issues. Not cutting my hair and choosing to do whatever I wanted to do was my rebellion, so she gave me a choice, either cut my hair or move out. I said, "Well, I'm moving out." I had this nice job and nowhere to go so I slept in my car in front of work for a week with just my clothes. Quite a different experience for me. Summer 1970 was in full effect, and a couple of nights were extremely warm. My car was a four-door, so I kept the front windows cracked and laid down on the back seat to get some rest. A week later I found a sleeping room for about twenty or thirty bucks a week. It had a refrigerator, but you had to mark everything or else risk someone taking it. I rarely ate there.

Shortly after the move I visited my eye doctor, Dr. Stamper in the city of Barnes, who informed me I would be blind within ten years. He told me I had Retinitis Pigmentosa, a disease that causes deterioration of the eyes. Within ten years of my diagnosis I would be blind. I didn't know there were varying levels to blindness. To me you could either see, or you were blind. Denial began to set in, and I conveniently tucked Dr. Stamper's diagnosis away in my subconscious until I was ready to deal with it. I walked back to my car and later unpacked my fate, spread it before me and thought about my future. I didn't see one. The first thing you think of is complete darkness in front of you. Next you think about your quality of life. I thought I'd never have a girlfriend or a great job. I thought about all the negatives and felt fully disgraced. Looking back at my dad as I worked with him around the house growing up, he'd say give me this screw driver and I'd hand him the wrong one and he'd say, "What are you, stupid? Grab the other one." I didn't realize I'd grabbed the wrong one. My parents never told me, nor my uncle Harry Mort who was an ophthalmologist! I look at some of the jobs I've had in my life like setting pins in a bowling alley at night. I'd set them up in the slot and jump up so I wouldn't get hit with the bowling pins. This was around 1966. I had lots of jobs. I started out with concessions, then I went to the bowling alley, then National Foods Grocery Store as a checker and stock boy. I was sixteen. I did Otties Pizza Parlor then Clark Oil as a gas attendant. When I graduated from high school, I drove a lunch truck because I was eighteen and I could get the chauffeurs' license. All my stops were memorized. I had my route committed to memory. I also worked at a drafting company in the shipping department then I moved into sales. On weekends I'd go to work at my stepfather's ornamental products shop. I was eighteen then.

BATS AND THE BOSTON BRUINS

In 1970, some friends got in a fight with the Boston Bruins at the Holiday Inn on Watson and Chippewa. We were hanging out with Joe and Craig. The four of us are in Craig's car and stop at Holiday Inn on Chippewa and Watson. One of the Boston Bruins is hanging out on the hotel bannister, so Joe hollers up and starts an argument with the guy. He challenges him to come down so we could kick his butt. There were four of us and there were about fifteen or twenty of them. They all start coming down. Joe opens the trunk and pulls out two baseball bats, one for Craig and one for him. They start this big rumble with the Boston Bruins and Mike, and I get out of there. We took off running. I ended up at this dance hall around the corner. There was a porch over the stairway as you walk in. I hid out there and Mike kept running. I don't even know where he went. The cops found me, and I told them I didn't know what they were talking about. I had to walk home about four or five miles.

My stepfather purchased my grandfather's house two blocks away and said he would rent it out to me. My friend David Ashley rented it with me. He had a motorcycle and we proceeded to start partying. We rode his motorcycle to a liquor store called 905. Lucky for us it was only five miles away. We walked in, got two cases of beer, and rode back on his motorcycle holding onto those two cases like they were gold at nineteen years old when drinking age was lawfully twenty-one years old. Back then wearing a helmet wasn't illegal, so I held onto both cases with one hand and hung onto the bike with the other. What a sight! This became an everyday ritual. Whoever came over, David's friends or mine, we'd sit there and drink beer. We never became alcoholics. We just partied and drank beer. One of my sister's girlfriends lived off Hampton on West Park. One day I went to visit and was introduced to her neighbors, the Kings. I met Dave King, Jeff King and Jared King. Now, Jeff had the ideal girlfriend, a five-piece drum set! I started going over Jeff's house almost every night. One night after playing the drums one of them pulled out a joint. Smoking a joint was going to be a first for me. I didn't even know how to hold it, so I held it like a cigarette. They were like, "No stupid, that's not how it's done." They had to teach me how to smoke it. That's how smoking pot entered the scene. I smoked about once a week with them. We would go get the beer, drink it and smoke a joint. Smoking weed became a weekend ritual and was never a problem. Our drinking and smoking lasted about three years.

Summer 1971 rolled around, and I was ready to take a nice break from work monotony. It was time for a much-needed vacation, so I took my first trip and hitchhiked to Florida. When I arrived at the bottom of the Georgia mountains, some guys I met warned me against being up there at night. I heeded their warning and was able to thumb a ride all the way down to Florida. The drive was so picturesque that I asked the driver to stop so I could take a picture of the Florida State sign. I still have that picture today. Danny said he wouldn't believe me unless he saw that sign.

I hitchhiked my way all the way to Jacksonville because the people I was hitchhiking with were going there. After crossing Florida's State line the guys I was riding with were going south so I said I'd go straight to the ocean. They let me out and I started walking on the highway hoping to catch a ride with someone new. One might find a walk on the highway uneventful. Not I. Soon after my pedestrian journey began, a curled-up rattlesnake appeared about five feet in front of me on my pathway. I stopped cold in my tracks and waited for car traffic to subside before running across the highway to the other side. If the snake stayed on his side and I on mine, we'd both be fine cause I wasn't going down without a fight. Boy, was I lucky I turned around to see that venomous critter when I did.

I continued walking for a little while, but nobody picked me up. I heard this rustling sound in the bushes. It was a wild boar! I pick up some rocks and throw them at this pig. That thing could have torn me up. Well, you know I was thinking it's just a pig, big deal. I didn't think about the fact that it was a wild animal.

Hitchhiking wasn't always dangerous, and I wasn't afraid at all. I wasn't worried because of my upbringing in learning how to fight fisticuffs. I was an expert at protecting myself because my dad taught me to fight. I made sure to sit next to the door so I could bail if need be and never had a problem. Having long hair made things easier. The guys pulled out a joint and we smoked on our way to wherever. We were hippies, that's what hippies did. That was hippie culture back then. We listened to country and rock music all the way to our destinations. I got rides from all kinds of people. Once with a couple of girls, another time with three cool rednecks. When I got to Jacksonville, a lady told me there were rooms available where she was staying. Since I didn't know where to go after arriving in Jacksonville, I decided to stay there for a couple of days. Jacksonville was different. There was no weed smoking, so everybody was straight. During the day, she and another guy showed me the city. The sun was so bright during the day I had to wear sunglasses and at night I couldn't see. The people I was staying with were Christians and I don't remember what denomination they were. On my last night they prayed over me. They held hands, spoke in tongues and tried to heal me. The next day I left and that was that. On my way back, with no maps, I knew which highways I needed to take. Before leaving I had charted my course, then stuck to it once on the road.

My vacation was two weeks. I didn't contact anyone from back home the entire time I was away, and folks were all worried. As I was making my way back to St. Louis in the second week, I mailed postcards to Denny and Pat's brother because they weren't believers. I guess I showed them. After I returned home, he confessed he was worried about me since he hadn't heard a peep for two weeks. He thought I was crazy for doing it, but he was probably respectfully envious if you ask me.

The following summer I decided to visit New Orleans. Of course, I hitchhiked and stayed two weeks. The third summer I travelled to Houston, TX and when I got back, my boss fired me. I'd only missed a few days at work. Someone brought me a sun lamp and stupid me kept it on for over two hours. I looked like a tomato and the pain I suffered was indescribable. So, I slept in the next morning or two. I didn't inform my boss I was sick, I just chose not to show up. A week or two after losing my job I went to Barnes during lunch hour. Everyone was gone and I sat in the office alone for a moment and broke down crying. The reality of Dr. Stamper's diagnosis and my fate finally hit me emotionally. Thoughts began whirling inside my head. I didn't want to accept the inevitable. What girl was going to want to go out with me? How was I going to find a good job and settle down? Every negative thought rose to the surface and I couldn't shake it, so I broke down. I had no one to counsel me or to talk to. I'm thankful that I never reached the point of suicide, but I do understand the low point people get to that makes them contemplate such a thing. Just because you bury things deep inside doesn't mean they aren't festering and won't resurface. We can only manage them to a point.

My father left a really good job at LaClede Gas Company at the same time he left my Mom. He started seeing this woman named Dorothy who helped him start his own company. She put everything in her name. He never received a paycheck, or so he says. He had it rough with this woman, hadn't even divorced my mother yet, and he paid no alimony.

Not until years later did I find out my grandfather was paying most of my Mom's bills. Here I was working myself into the ground at eleven years old and her bills were being paid. I believed my Mom truly did not like me because I reminded her of my Dad. She would never admit it though. My older sister hated me too.

My father died on March 18, 1987, the same date my brother Eugene was born. His funeral was a wreck and I was an armed guard. My mom, who absolutely hated him, attended. His second wife sat in the pews near the lady whose house he died in. My job was to make certain the three of them stayed far away from each other. I was running around like crazy. My mom wanted to go to the funeral and was the happiest woman in the world when he died. She wanted to celebrate, and she did. He had a heart attack in his girlfriend's house. He tried to get out the door so he wouldn't die in her house, but he didn't make it. To be perfectly honest, he was trying to get out of the house because he was married not because he didn't want her to have that horrible memory. He collapsed in the living room and died instantly.

Right before I left for Florida, I got into it with my stepfather. My sister Barb was renting an apartment about three miles from the house in Hampton Gardens and he'd gone over there. When I talked to her the next night, she told me she was very upset with him. I confronted him at my Mom's house when he got off work. My sister never told me what happened, but I had a keen sense he was sexually inappropriate with her. He was a bricklayer. That day he pulled out this four-foot level, approximately two inches wide and made of solid steel. He held it firm like a baseball bat and said, "If you come near me, I'm going to knock your head off." I stayed my distance while cussing at him. All of this happened on the front lawn.

Lucky was Mom's second husband. His real name was Harvey Flare. He made a handsome salary as a bricklayer and would take my Mom on trips to Las Vegas and other nice places. She was not going to lose this Golden Goose. He would tell me, "Don't get close, I'll knock your head off." Lucky was big, but he understood I was not a weakling either. I had no fear and would have faced him toe to toe without a bit of hesitation. If you fear someone, your chances of getting hurt increase. So, I never feared anyone I went up against. I warned him that he better not go back over to my sister's house again, and he listened.

The room I stayed in was in a boarding house. After living in that room for a while, my grandfather's house became available. He was placed in a retirement center. Lucky took over the house and rented it out to me. That's when I got my roommate Dave in 1970. One Christmas, we decided to make a pyramid out of beer cans we'd drunk from, so you can imagine how big it was. We did this between Thanksgiving and New Year's Eve. It was like an art project. We stacked them in the corner of the living room while Lucky was out of town. Our pyramid was looking great when all of a sudden Lucky calls and says, "I'll be down there in about an hour." We were like, "Oh my gosh if he sees this, he's going to kill us!" So, we grabbed the beer cans and started throwing them in the closet. There were so many beer cans we could barely shut the closet door.

One night Lucky snuck down to the house. We were hanging out in the kitchen next to a screened in porch. Lucky stands at the screen door watching Denny smoke a joint and runs around the side of the house to the front door. Fuming mad, he bursts inside and starts yelling at Denny calling him a beady-eyed SOB. Man, we've experienced some pretty crazy moments. Party time was simply drugs and beer. We didn't care about going to the clubs and dancing.

FRAN

When I met Fran in the fall of 1972, I was skinny with a twenty-nine inch waist. I didn't weigh over one hundred fifty-five pounds but was solid as a rock. At twelve years old, I carried three ninety-pound bags of ice in my arms as part of my job. While I was in the Boy Scouts, I bought this spring piece of equipment that stretches your arms and feet. Using these things over a period of time helped me build strength and stamina.

One night at the house we were partying with this girl named Louise. She lived with Fran, and I was trying to date her. She wouldn't date me because I was going blind. Her philosophy was I'd never be able to provide for her, so we just hung out together. We went to bars and I was like her protector. How interesting is that? I'm the guy who couldn't see going to bars as her protector, but she wouldn't date me because I was blind. When we would arrive at the bar, she'd find someone else to hang out with.

We went to the Southern Illinois University Carbondale which hosted summer festivals. There was always a massive crowd. One summer we went to see Earth, Wind & Fire and a couple of other bands. After one of the concerts, we went back to Louise's house and her roommate Fran was there. Fran was also married to a guy named Charlie who I later became friends with.

I soon learned that Charlie was a manic depressive who had a drinking problem and would come home drunk to terrorize Fran and her daughter Sharon. Prior to our meeting each other I heard Charlie came home one night while Fran was pregnant, threw her on a table and threatened to cut the baby out of her belly. She had him thrown in jail.

I began to come around more often and noticed the basement floor was tore up because the soil pipe was cracked open. Rats had gotten into the house and Fran had to hire an exterminator. I finally got fed up with Charlie, pulled all the pipes out of the ground and threw them in the backyard. I looked at him and said, "Now you have to do something!" He was rather ticked off with me, but so what! I didn't care that he was six foot three. I got all new pipes and told him let's go to it and put them back in. Some of the lead fell off the pipe so he threw it back in the pod. That is something you don't do! It exploded and we both were burned.

On February 23, 1973, Fran's daughter turned six years old. That night she and her kids stayed at my apartment. We were just friends. Louise came by and cleared all my friends out. There was to be no pot in the apartment whatsoever.

I moved out of Lucky's house because he was going to sell it and rented an apartment six blocks down the hill from him. That was the first time Fran came over. I wasn't trying to date her or anything and had a girlfriend at the time. On Mother's Day I slept on the couch in the living room and gave her and the kids the two beds. That's how it all started. Fran fell in love with me in October and I broke up with my girlfriend. She still needed a place of refuge away from Charlie. He finally left, but before doing so he came over to her house one night, took all the dishes out of the cabinets and broke them throughout the house. He was the ultimate loser. He left in October.

On November 1, 1973, a buddy of mine who later became my brother-in-law decides he's going to go out to California. I was up for the impromptu trip, so we head out to Hermosa Beach, CA for a week and a half. He decides to let me drive going out there because he needed a nap. So, I took over and drove for five minutes before pulling over because I couldn't see! That was the end of that. I felt bad, but we both respected our lives and were not looking forward to becoming roadkill. Each day was harder than the first to come back to St. Louis. We were having one heck of a party. We were raided by the police one night at this guy's house because of our partying and playing music too loud. We were in the garage with the door wide open. Hey, we thought we sounded great and even recorded a song named "Give Me Your Gravy" but never did anything with it.

It was time to head back to St. Louis and a guy we met named John asked if he could come back with us. He had lived in St. Louis but moved out to L.A. following his girlfriend at the time. She got married to someone else, so he wanted a ride back home with us. When we start making our way back, we got four flat tires, four different times!

It was close to Thanksgiving when we arrived back in St. Louis and I had to immediately start work on the house. Charlie had messed up the furnace, so my Dad had to come fix it. I'd been working for him until I returned from L.A. When I went back to the workplace my dad took a hammer to me. He was very upset because of the wig I had been wearing while working for him.

It was a friend's idea first. My Dad didn't realize I had been wearing it for four months. He finally noticed the morning I came back to work. My own hair was sticking out from underneath the wig.

Fran and I were still dating and doing goofy romantic things to keep the magic in our relationship. When Christmas time rolled around, I moved in with her because Charlie had been harassing and scaring her by coming to her house. He came by on Christmas Day with a toy for Chuck but didn't even have a dollar to buy batteries so he could play with it. I said something to him and followed him out the door. He proceeds to tell me off. I let him say whatever he had to say before he took off. Similar scenarios played out over the next six months. I'm working for a tree service with Marty and John and we decide to go into this bar for lunch. Guess who is sitting at the bar. Charlie starts mouthing off saying he hadn't been in a good bar room brawl in four years. He's going on and on for fifteen minutes and I'm eating my lunch just waiting for him. We're sitting right by the door and he comes walking past me. I couldn't resist the urge to say, "Hey, why don't you send your old lady some money?" He said two foul words and with that I knocked the chair over and ran out the door to catch up with him. We are running through the parking lot which is downhill. Halfway down he's trying to get in his car, and I start cussing him out. I called him every cuss word in the book and some in Italian at least twice and begged him to hit me. I was waiting for it because I didn't want to be the problem of Fran's divorce. This goes on for ten minutes while his girlfriend is threatening to call the police. Finally, I told him I was wasting my breath, called him a big chicken and start turning around to go back to the bar when he punches me in the nose. With lightning speed, I picked him up and threw him over the hood of his car. Mind you he is six foot three. Everybody's at the top of the hill watching as he and I roll down. I jump on him and start smacking him in the face. All you can hear is his wimp voice begging, "I give, I give, I give!" I was beating the crap out of him and finally grabbed his head to pound it in the ground. I slipped my arm out from beneath his head and the guys at the top of the hill said they got a headache watching it. Charlie was dazed. That's when he quit and said, "Man I quit, I'm done, please let go!" So, I let him up. One could see he was off-balance. For the road I said, "Here's your sucker punch back," and I punched him right in the nose. One of the guys I was with found my glasses and since I was three blocks away from my house I walked home. I was done for the day. I walk in the house with blood on my shirt and Fran starts laughing like crazy. Between laughter she said, "I know what happened." She knew I kicked Charlie's butt. Then she asked me, "How does the other guy look?" I said,

"Dazed and confused." She never feared him again. He moved out of town and was later arrested spending years in jail.

He finally decided to file for divorce from Fran but chose to hire the same lawyer she had. Because of that things became messy and it took what seemed an eternity for it to be final. The divorce was final in January 1976 and we waited several days before deciding to get married. We happily tied the knot on May 26th. I didn't want to wait a long time to get married for the kid's sake. They went to a Catholic School and living together was considered unacceptable in the 70s. They were also able to say that they had a Mom and Dad. Various circumstances determined that my partying days were over. I found a better and more expensive apartment. Fran needed refuge on the weekends, and I lost my job. It was time for me to get serious and make changes.

CHAPTER SEVEN

I Can Do It

After quitting my job at the gas company, I decided to try college. The fact I was going blind coupled with not knowing what I was going to do with my life was depressing, so I decided to jump into student life feet first. At the beginning of spring session, I enrolled in two courses; basic music and one other course. Having no idea what I'd major in, I thought music might work. Believe it or not, I survived Missouri School for the Blind aka Vocational Rehabilitation. Voc Rehab paid for my education. I was getting paid to go to school each month, received a benefit and my schooling was all paid for. I earned two A's which surprised the heck out of me. As it turned out, I enjoyed school and learning.

I began studying full-time at Forest Park Community College and attended a few additional Junior colleges during summer sessions. At Forest Park, I took nineteen credit hours per semester. My subjects were class piano, class woodwinds, stream class, percussion class and music theory. Five classes per semester that were mostly music was very easy for me. I had never been trained musically. Never! I could pick up an instrument and start playing it instantly. I know it sounds a bit farfetched but that's how it worked for me. I later came to understand I was divinely gifted and at the time paid it little attention. I never had musical training until I went to college and graduated top five in my class with an Associate Degree in Music.

Life brings its rewards but can also throw a curve ball causing you to step out of bounds. Distractors have a way of showing up when you are trying to excel in life.

It was summer 1974. Two friends and I were traveling in my car to a buddy's house in Des Peres, MO. Marty was driving, I sat in the middle seat, John rode shotgun and all our instruments were stowed in the trunk. As Marty was exiting the Manchester off ramp, we got creamed in the rear by a guy who wasn't paying any attention to the road. It all happened so quickly. I bent down to grab a beer as my face collided with the windshield and mirror right above my eyes. My back was miserably hurt, and the impact enhanced the progression of my loss of eyesight. The driver responsible for the accident was clearly in the wrong, but unfortunately I wasn't allowed to initiate the topic of my impairment in court. The opposing attorney did provide a moment for me to explain my ailment. My attorney was trying to signal me to speak up, but I could not see his gestures and the moment passed. Though we won the case, we weren't awarded as much had I testified.

In August and September of 1974, I started teaching drum and bugle corps at Roe and Oak elementary schools. One day I needed to purchase drum supplies and walked into the Kennedy-Browning Music Store to purchase a cymbal. While there, I asked if they could use a drum teacher. I thought, "Hey, if Glen Papa Wright can do it, so can I!" The owner, Mr. Kennedy, said yes and hired me instantly!

Ray Kennedy was a nice, kind, soft spoken and trustworthy man who sent me students and helped build my first clientele. He had two sons, Ray and Tom Kennedy, who were a few years younger than me but well established. They played with Dave Weckel, a famous drummer who played with Chick Corea. Ray and Tom have toured Europe and Asia and are highly revered in the jazz world. This is how my career as a private teacher began and I am indebted to Mr. Kennedy forever.

As Mr. Kennedy grew older, he became worried about his health and could no longer handle the day-to-day operations of the business. He offered me the opportunity to purchase and become the new owner of his music store, but I was already working with the St

Louis public school system and had great insurance that covered my entire family. At the time, I didn't believe his offer was the wise choice for me as I could no longer see. I certainly hated to disappoint him. He has long since passed away, but his sons and I remain very good friends to this day.

In 1975, I continued with school and teaching, and all was going quite well. Then a curve ball in the way of new neighbors moved into the neighborhood through the HUD system, the Young family. A brother and sister married each other and bore children. Pure, unadulterated incest. Their first child was a girl who was born normal. The children that followed were all mentally challenged and mongoloids. Sadly, they were a bad element on our street. They vandalized the beverage and food machines in the building and harassed the elderly people to give them money. These kids would walk right up to their homes and threaten to break their windows if they didn't comply.

Since they never really bothered me, I left them alone. They eventually tried to pull one of my daughters into the alley to rape her, but she kicked them and got away. When I found out, I could no longer turn a blind eye. I got the call and immediately started running toward home until a bus came. I hopped on the bus then jumped off about sixteen blocks from the house and continued running from there. When I got home the police were called. I couldn't wait for them to arrive and went over to their house, grabbed the kid and dragged him out on the front porch. His dad came running around the front with a pair of hand snips used for trimming grass. I had his son by the throat up against the porch wall and said, "If you move one inch, you will be wearing those scissors. Drop them right where you're standing!" He did. The police pulled up and said I was wrong for grabbing the kid, but I didn't care. He was lucky the cops pulled up when they did because I was going to put his head through the brick wall.

It wasn't right, but one of the kids on our block threw a brick through their window believing if this family didn't have constant air conditioning, they wouldn't stay. These kids tried burning down their own garage at least three or four times. The fire fighters got tired of coming to stomp out their little campfires. So, on the fourth call they received, the fire department burned it down themselves believe it or not. The whole thing was just bad. These kids would literally rape their sisters out in the alley. I was determined to rid them from our neighborhood.

My house needed a new roof. One afternoon while I was working on it, a sergeant from 2nd District pulled up and said, "Hey, hey, come here. I want to talk to you." I climbed down from the roof and met him on the sidewalk. He continued, "I just wanted to let you know if something happened where a Molotov cocktail found its way into their basement and the house caught fire, we would not investigate." That's how badly the police wanted them out. We all wanted them out!

I should not boast, but I felt we had no choice. They threatened the neighbors. They broke in and drilled holes in my basement door just to see what was inside. I had to put steel plates over the panels so they couldn't see in. I added a steel bar across the door on two hinges so they couldn't kick the door in.

One of the neighborhood kids was on his racing bike flying down the street with a brick in his hand. He threw the brick into the back windshield of their car as he rode by. That's how badly the neighborhood wanted him out. A cop comes and blames me for it. In my anger, I tell the cop, "I'm tired of this! This guy blames me for everything!" I'm going off on the cop and he tells me to calm down, "Mr. Guzman we didn't say you did anything. We just wanted to see if you knew who did." In the meantime, they were outside screaming, hollering and cussing at the cops. He looks up and sees a street sign that says no parking on Fridays from 9:00 to noon and writes him a ticket for being parked in the wrong spot. As he hands the ticket to him, he says, "Have a good day," and walks away. After the cop told me what I could do by throwing a Molotov cocktail through the basement window, I decided we had to be more extreme in our approach. We could not burn them out. So, my neighbor who was also one of my drum students and I started pounding the heck out of my drums. We were so loud that a couple of neighbors said their pictures were falling off the walls. We kept it going for fifteen minutes straight. I also learned that others on the block climbed on top of their roof with axes and chopped holes in it. Unfortunately, these extreme measures seemed to be the only way to get them out of the neighborhood and they finally worked. Their oldest sister wasn't affected at birth. She was a social worker and had them placed in a rehabilitation hospital facility where they remained for a month. They really needed to be in some sort of long-term facility or asylum.

Oft times when you make a commitment to accomplish great goals to make something of your life, great challenges find their way to you. These neighbors were unwittingly used to try and dismantle my educational pursuits. It felt almost like a sci-fi movie. Beings from outer space landed next door on a mission to destroy and take over. Sometimes you must be aggressive. I'm not encouraging anyone to do anything illegal or physically harmful. Absolutely not! But it may take more than a simple reprimand to get a job done. Our community came together and did just that.

CHAPTER EIGHT
TEACHING BLIND

It's January 1978, school was revving up after winter break and I was the new student teacher on board. There were many band directors who tried to teach these kids but didn't know what they were doing in percussion. This was typical for St. Louis Public Schools, which made me one of the most sought-after instructors. I entered the classroom with ten kids present and Mutiny on the Bounty knocked me hard on the chin. These young, very confident and bold students told me they were not going to study with me until I showed them how good I was. I told them, "I'm sorry, but I'm the teacher. Sit down and be quiet." They didn't love me saying that at all and repeated their disgruntled statement, "We are not going to listen to anything you say until you prove to us that you can play and that you know what you are doing!" Laval Belle was one of these less than impressed students. They further explained that they'd had teachers who came in and couldn't teach the class anything and they were tired of it. Secretly, I agreed but couldn't show my hand. I turned to Laval and said, "Alright, put your snare drum right there and bring one over here for me." I had to be in full command and he respectfully did what I asked. I continued, "Laval, do you want to play match grip or traditional?" Match grip is where you make a fist, and your thumb sticks out providing a space for the drumstick to lie. Both hands are in the same position, hence the term, "Match Grip." "Traditional Grip" is where your right hand is right side up and the left hand is upside down. The thumb and two fingers, down and the first finger lays across the top. Laval thought he'd be smart and say traditional. Well, I already knew I was a badass drummer because my first teacher ever on drums was Glenn Papa Wright who I vowed to smoke with my playing. I ended up teaching him Theory and Marimba two years later. I knew I had Laval but played dumb for a few minutes. I already had this in the bag! We set the two drums up and I said, "We'll go open to close." He said, "What's that?" I said, "Slow to fast." He answered, "Oh, okay." So, we start out and we're chucking. I had a beat going, two rights and two lefts, then I sped up a little. Then he sped up a little. I let him keep speeding up until he started to lose the beat a little and couldn't go any faster. That was my cue to leap in and let it rip. He had to give up, stop playing and just watch. He surrendered with, "I'm ready to learn."

Laval ended up coming to my house once a week to take private drum lessons and did really well. He grew to become one of the baddest drummers for over forty decades, playing all over the world for many popular celebrities and foreign royalty. When he's in town, he still visits the house and we reminisce about those days and how my wife cooked him his favorite childhood delicacy, franks and beans.

I was substitute teaching at University City High School as one of my first teaching jobs. One day I was sitting at my desk taking roll and a kid says to me, "What if I hit you?" I told him, "Well, it won't be good for you because I'm a black belt and army trained." Sometimes you must outdo the enemy. You must be quick and even quicker on your feet. I really do have two belts, that's no lie or embellishment. I do not know where they are now, it has been so many years.

Again, while was taking roll on my second day teaching at Beaumont, a student five feet from me on my left called me a "Honky MF." I turned to him and said, "You can't talk like that. You are going to have to leave the room please." He proceeded to tell me that he didn't have to do sh** and to keep my f-ing mouth shut. I repeated that he needed to leave the room please. Note that I used the word please. He proceeded to tell me to shut the f up again. As I walked over toward his direction, I kicked the chair from underneath him then grabbed him so he would not get hurt. Then I said, "Now, you are going to leave the room," and I personally escorted him out of the room. He ran to a school counselor, Moses Jones, and five minutes later he called and said I needed to come to his office. I told him I had a class, he said he knew and was sending someone down to watch my students. I went to his office and he tried to tell me what the student said about me kicking the chair from underneath him. Now, he wanted to hear my version of what happened. I told him I was walking toward him as he was falling out of the chair and caught him so he would not get hurt. Then I escorted him out of the room. Moses asked the student to wait in the hall and close the door. He beckoned me to lean over his desk and underneath his breath informed me that this boy's brother shot a teacher last year and needed my class to graduate. He then asked, "What are we going to do?" I said suspend him the rest of the week, but he must come back and apologize. On Monday, the student returned and when I realized he was in class I told him he had to apologize. He leaned over and quietly said, "I'm sorry Mr. G." I said, "That is not good enough. Stand up and tell the class." As he addressed the class his right arm was raised upward and he said, "If any of you mother..." Then he stopped himself and rephrased his sentence using a better choice of words, "If anyone gives Mr. G. any trouble you'll have to answer to me!"

My philosophy was I wouldn't curse like the kids were used to hearing. The guy I replaced used to curse. After parade competitions, he would go out and buy a trophy then lie and tell the kids they won the Martin Luther King Parade or whatever parade it was.

I had no training on how to teach the band because I was so new at all of this. The first football game comes and it's pouring down rain outside. Fran is driving to Beaumont and she notices that streets are flooded and did not know what to do. She was afraid to drive through all the water. The first football game gets rained out and we must turn around. The game was in North St. Louis where they do not use trash pickup. They use the sewers and they were all backed up. It was a mess! Fran pulls over and I take over driving. She said it was a scary ride out of the neighborhood, but she allowed it. I got us out of the flood waters, and she took over after we were on dry land. I only drove about two to four blocks.

The football game was postponed, and the next home game was a week or two away. The kids were trying to be good and obnoxious at the same time. There was a kid named James Browden. Lucy was his nickname and he ran the band. He was short and in his fifth year. He had to attend school for an extra semester. He is running everything or at least trying to. Their previous teacher would take them out after the games or parades and buy a couple cases of beer and pot and smoke and drink with them. That's why he was relieved from his job. He told the kids to give me hell because this "honky" was coming in and taking him away from what was rightfully his. I had already told myself I would not cuss no matter what.

We're going to the first game. I didn't really know how to teach marching band, yet I was learning quick. We didn't have to march this game and just sat in the bleachers. While we were sitting there, I tell the kids we were going to play a song. I start the count down, "1, 2, 3" then I hear someone say, "don't play." I threw the baton down on the first count and not a sound came out of the horn section. Nothing! I try it again, "1, 2, 3." Still nothing. By then the football teams are ready to go and we couldn't play. The next time we got the ball the same thing happened. We were going to play a little short part of the song to entertain the masses. I count down, "1, 2, 3" and it happened again! Now the audience was laughing at me, so I climb all the way up to the back bleachers and, believe me, it was trouble getting up there. I confront Lucy right there in the stands and order him to take his drum off. He says, "What?" "I said take your drum off." He said, "You can't do that!" I told him, "I SAID, shut up and take your drum off or do you want me to take it off?" He starts grumbling and mumbling and I say, "Now give me your overlay." That is what goes over the coat. He takes it off. Then I told him to get out of the bleachers. I shouted, "This is my band!" He disrobed, walked out, and I had no trouble after that.

It is time to go home. Lucy is standing by the bus as if he is preparing to get on, but what he is really doing is telling his friends he was going to stall us. I told the bus driver, "Shut the door and let's go!" The bus driver was a bit surprised and said, "What?" I repeated, "Shut the door!" We left Lucy at the football game. When he arrives back to school, I meet him outside to let him know he was not allowed in the band room anymore and he was kicked out of the band. I kicked him out because he caused so much trouble for me. That was my first football game ever. He was the right-hand man to the teacher I replaced, so he looked at me as the dumb white guy. All kinds of trouble came that following Monday. He and his mom came up to school. The principal didn't know a thing about what happened at the football game so I gladly I told him the entire story. Lucy chimed in with the sorry excuse, "Well, he left me at the game." I replied, "You didn't get on the bus. Money for the bus is coming out of my budget and we couldn't wait another half an hour for you to finish talking to all your friends. So, we left. You didn't get on the bus like everybody else, so you know, that was your problem." His mother said I was picking on him. The principal asked me what I did about it and I told him I threw the young man out of the band. The principal went on to say, "Well, yeah he's been in the band for four years and he's going to graduate in January." I said, "Not from the band." The principal, Mr. Cozy Marks, Jr., agreed with me. So, I mastered the first hurdle.

I was about twenty-seven years old at the time and it was 1978. I didn't know what I was doing. The previous band director was gone but was still trying to run the band. He had made Lucy the drum major, but I didn't care. Lucy was out of the band. He was not going to tell the kids not to play and they listen to him on my watch! He had too much authority. I was the one in charge and if I said play, the band should play. We argued for about ten minutes and though his mother threatened me, I didn't budge an inch. She slightly threatened me saying, "Well you know you're in our neighborhood!" She put an accent on the word "hood" and tried to scare me saying that I'd never know what could happen. I said, "That's right, but you know what? I'm not worried about it." She was shocked and said, "What?" I repeated myself, "I'm not worried about it." She thought she could scare me off and cause me to fear. So, later on the kids started asking me, "Where is your ride, your big car?" We were driving a 1963 Chevy Nova two-door and these kids were asking me where was my Cadillac. Laughable! I told them I didn't have another car, but they didn't believe me. I got tired of them asking so one day I told them I had a Corvette sitting at home and didn't want to drive it up here. That shut them up. It was a big lie, but it worked and made them stop asking.

We made it through football season, and parade season began. The principal told us to leave our classroom door unlocked and I was the only dummy that listened to him. Everyday some kid opened the door and turned the lights on and off. The light switch was right next to the door. There were no windows because they were all boarded up. Two years before I had gotten there some kids firebombed the band room, so they boarded all the windows. I had a huge exhaust fan in the ceiling that kept the room cool. There was no air conditioning, but the fan did help. I was constantly arguing with the students. They were trying to show me who was boss. Around September, the principal tells us there is a PTA meeting and the teachers should be present. So, Fran and I went and parked our '63 Nova in front of the meeting place. We walked inside for the meeting and Fran is chosen to be the stenographer. We were the only teachers there. Maybe five parents came so that was our last time attending. When we got to our car to go home, I found my car battery was stolen and had to call a friend for help. He came with a battery, installed it for use, so we were able to drive home. So, that's how much the students liked me. But I was hard on them you know, and so after the PTA meeting rolled around, they kept opening my door and slamming the lights. When the lights would go out and the room went black, the kids started throwing music stands. This was a real test for me, but I always made it to the lights quickly to turn them on and I'd say, "So and so, put that music stand down." It was bad until Christmas season. One day this kid decides he's going to come in and flicker the lights and take off running. I was done with this foolishness. The kids didn't know that I ran track in high school. So, I go running after this kid and I'm on his heels. He goes up the staircase all the way to the third floor and I'm on the third floor following him. I say, "Is that the fastest you can run, come on you've got to run faster than that I'm on your heels, dude." The next thing I know something hits the ground and slides down the hall. Well, I didn't know the guard was following us, so he stops and picks up the guy's pocketknife and I finally gave up saying, "I was tired." I let him keep running and walked back to my room. At that point the kids were having a heyday hollering and screaming when I walked in. I said, "Is that the fastest you guys can run?" They were like, "No we can run, we sure can!" I'm giving them all this trouble back. I was teaching the jazz band at this point when the kid interrupted us. Two guys, Robert Gobel, and I can't think of the other guy's name, came out of the band room closet where the instruments were and sat down. Twelve guys in the class kept disrupting and I was so ticked I kicked my shoes off and slid them over to the wall where I could find them again. Then I drop down in my karate stance and said, "Make a circle." Oh I had their attention now. They shut up. We had locks at the top of the doors, so I took the padlock off my locker and locked the front door. The back door was already locked. For the first time, I cussed. I said, "I'm tired of all your bull****. I told you to make a circle" They asked me why they needed to make a circle. I said, "Cuz I'm going to knock the s*** out of all of you!" I squatted down and said, "Come on! You guys think you're big well let's see how big you are." This is all true, but it's not documented anywhere. They were saying, "Hey man, you're crazy!" I said, "You know, come on there's twelve of you." They said, "You're Mr. G!" I said, "Come on, come on, come on!" They finally decided they weren't going to give me anymore trouble. With that, I unlock the door and five minutes later the bell rings, and they all took off.

The two guys that had been in the closet decided they were going to steal two flutes, but they didn't take the cases. I check the instruments every single day. The next morning when I go in to work, a policeman had caught this one guy and brought him in. The kid told the cop that I gave him the flute. The day the flute was stolen he was wearing a suit. The police stopped him while he was walking home and noticed the flute sticking out of his pocket thinking it might be a gun. The officer asked him where he'd gotten the flute and he told him I had given it to him. In spite of the kid's story, they confiscated the flute. The following morning, they brought him to me and said, "We've got the flute back and we're letting him off the hook." I said, "No you're not, he stole the flute, and you need to have them arrested!" The cop answered, "No. No, we don't need to do that. We got the flute back." I said, "Yeah, I know but he stole the flute. Earlier I had checked both flute cases and found them to be light in weight. When I opened them up, the flutes were not there." I needed to have this kid arrested to make the strong point that I am not going to tolerate his behavior, and neither would the school. The policeman would not let it go and said, "Look, I got the flute back and we're not going to prosecute." I said, "Alright, are you through with this flute?" He said, "Right, yes, we got the flute back. I tested it and it works okay." I said, "Are you sure we're not going to prosecute him for stealing this flute?" He replied, "Yeah." I said "Alright. Well, officer, arrest him because he stole two flutes." As soon as those words fell from my mouth the kid confesses, "I didn't steal the second one, Robert Gobel did." Just like that he gave him up. The cop asked where Robert was and I politely told them, he is in the band room. So the cop says, "Well, let's go down and pick him up. We walk down to the basement. I open these double doors and what I found was priceless. There is Robert Gobel and two other guys puffing on a joint. One guy says, "There's two of them and three of us, let's take them." Robert says, "That's Mister G. I ain't messing with him." We picked up twenty-two joints off of them. The boys gave them to the cop and the cop gave all of them to Moses Jones. When the cop comes back to get them from Moses there are only fifteen. Another cop said to me, "Didn't I give you twenty-two?" Moses said, "Oh, no sir, you only gave me fifteen." This is what I was up against. They took Robert to his Mom who was a teacher at Beaumont and released him to her. I told him he couldn't come back to the band room because he stole two flutes. He was a great drummer and was furious with me. I banned him from the orchestra forever. I had to do that to make an example so no one else would act in the same way. They needed to see that I was serious. That's just one day!

There were days that were worse. Kids would set trash cans on fire and roam the halls. They cussed at the teachers using extremely foul language and felt no remorse. Sometimes they would even take a swing at me. Kids from other schools would come to our school with booze in their pockets. I remember one day coming home and going straight to bed, no dinner, no nothing. I went to bed and slept it off until the next day. I'd had my fill because of everything that had gone on up to that point it. It wasn't easy, it wasn't pleasant, and I wasn't seeing well. So, I was a little worried about things. This was happening before Christmas vacation. When we returned to school after the break, Robert Gobel is not in the band and he wouldn't be around for a while. It looked like the rest of the year would be smooth sailing. Well, it wasn't. Later that year, a kid that didn't belong in my class is in the band room with a flute. He said he just came by to pick up a flute, but he doesn't have a case. I asked him to let me see his flute. When he handed it to me, I showed him the flute didn't belong to our school.

He said, so what are you doing with my flute? I told him he couldn't have it and would contact the band director at Sumner High School, and he could pick it up. He grabs the flute and I never let go. We're pulling it back and forth for five minutes straight. I was squeezing the keys and he was too, and I got tired. My forearms are big, so I finally said the heck with it, let go and he flies backwards. I take the lock off of my locker, lock the door and call the guard. I told the guard I had a trespasser with a stolen flute, and they needed to come and pick him up. He says, "Okay, Mr. G, I'll be right down." He comes down and picks the kid up. I told the class, "You do the crime, you have to pay the time." That was a quote from the actor who played Barretta in the popular television series back in the day. For the rest of the school year people got the idea not to mess with me and gave me the nick name of "Barretta" which I wore proudly.

In May 1978, the students decided to mess with me. One kid lit my hair on fire, but it didn't burn long, and I put it out with my hand. The next hour I get a phone call from my good friend Haji who had heard about the incident. He was calling to check on me. I reassured him I was fine. I knew somebody snitched, so now my reputation was changing. The kids were beginning to like me now. So, it took about a year to settle in where no one continued to bother me. I went through my initiation and lived through it. I was on a mission to prove that I was the boss. It was tough!

Robert Gobel thoroughly hated me. He graduated that year and wanted to graduate with the band. His stupidity kept him from doing so and he remained quite upset about it years later.

In the 1981-82 season, I took Beaumont to the Dallas Cardinal game. Preparing for that game was a lot of work including after-school rehearsals. We were quickly approaching game day. I told the band there was going to be a Saturday morning practice, and no one would be excused. They told me they were not going to do it. "We don't have a choice!" I said. Time was short and they had to learn the routines for the halftime show. They said, "Yeah we do." They were boasting about it. I said, "Alright, I'll tell you what, I'll challenge you." I challenged them to do one lap around the track. If they won, they didn't have to come to the Saturday rehearsal. If I won, they would have to show up. They agreed to my challenge because they thought I would surely lose. Everybody had to run and we all had to take off at the same time. Mr. Marks was the judge and was waiting for us outside after school to give us the count. On the word GO, we took off! There were eighty or more kids running the football field track. We run around the first turn and I'm already halfway through. We are running down the second leg, picking up steam and getting close to coming around the second turn. There are only three guys in front of me. I passed the third guy, the second guy was in front of me by about ten steps. As I'm passing him, he jerks and throw me off. Now we are coming up on Robin, the girl who was in the lead and she's only ten steps ahead of me. I would have passed her, but a kid ran in front of me and blocked me. When it was over, they knew that their win was unfair because they cheated. They asked me, "Mr. G do you really think you could have taken Robin?" I exclaimed, "Yes!" Well, they all showed up on Saturday morning. My guardian angel was working over overtime.

The principal became a good friend. We worked in cahoots with each other to focus the kids on success. You must be creative and imaginative when it comes to corralling students around your cause. I am not like some teachers who will just hang up the hat and say I'm not doing this or that because they are not getting paid to struggle with kids. The fact that I did, and did not have to, built trust between me and my students. I grew up the hard way and had no one to teach me. From the time I was twelve, everything I did I had to do on my own. That is how I learned that no one is going to do it for you. You must work hard for yourself. I did not rely on anyone.

Right before Thanksgiving 1981, we went to the Dallas St. Louis Cardinals game and I took one hundred fifty kids. I added my daughter Sharon and her friend to the flute line. I told the whole group that during the second quarter nobody was to leave their seat. They were all in heaven on the field with these huge football players they thought they were so great. Second quarter comes, they are all in their seats. I am feeling, my gosh the principal and all the assistant principals and a bunch of other teachers all got tickets for the game! We had to be great to make them proud! We did an excellent job and they asked us back for the following season. I'm sure we made them immensely proud.

It was getting dark and hard for me to see where I was going while trying to exit the field. We were at Busch Stadium and I was behind the drum major. I had no idea how I was going to get back to my seat because it was dark outside. The whole band passed me by, and he was the last one off. The thought came as clear as a bell, "Grab his hand, hold it up high and walk off the field in victory." I grabbed his hand and held it up like victors and walked off the field. The drum major did not know he was keeping me safe as he helped me back to my seat.

Little did I know that evening I would not return to take part in the next event as their band teacher. 1982 was a rough year. In June, all the music and fine arts teachers were laid off and my sole income was gone just like that. Serious concern arose because I had three children and a wife to support, but struggle was not foreign to me. That hard-working ten-year-old kid who struggled to put himself through private school all by himself, rose and adjusted his thinking cap. Let me not diminish the fact I had also been teaching privately at Drum Headquarters in 1981. So, I was not completely without means, although more money was certainly necessary to support my family.

Surprisingly, at the same time 1982-83 became one of the most prosperous years of my life. Yes, I had gotten laid off and, yes, I was placed in a school that was a waste of time for me at least, but I also started my own business. I had my own music studio. My back porch was remodeled, I bought a better car and a better piano on top of that! I had an upright model made in 1910. I also was able to get a brand new drum set. I mean I got everything I needed through the School for the Blind. I was sorry I could not have gotten a better education at the school. I'll tell you more about that in the following chapter.

I was hired again at Blewett Middle School in 1983. Unfortunately, I knew I couldn't function well there because I would be jeopardizing Fran's health by having her take me back and forth alone. She was already doing so much for me. As fate would have it, I met a woman who had a little clout in our city. I taught her son privately and we developed a nice camaraderie. She knew people in some high places. So, I called her one day and asked if she could aid me in finding a teaching position in South St. Louis. This kind woman referred me to a wonderful work opportunity as a teacher at Melanphy Middle School. I was so appreciative that I surprised her with one dozen roses to say thank you.

In 1991, I decided our band would play "Prelude in C Minor by Rachmaninoff." These young musicians are sixth, seventh, and eighth grade middle school students. Nevertheless, they were good enough to play that song. I had vowed never to play that song again because in 1982 the Beaumont High School band played it in concert, and I got laid off. All of the liberal arts departments were laid off. The entire school was closed as a matter of fact. Then again in 1991, I was laid off after playing the same song. So, I vowed to never play that song again. Yes, be it a silly superstition or an over-zealous bad omen, that song would never be part of my repertoire again.

But here I am, it's 1991 and I have another group of young musicians. I couldn't believe the quality of musicianship I was getting out of these kids because Melanphy Middle School was a dumping ground. I'm getting laid off again, but this time I knew about it one month ahead of time. The kids were already set, and I knew what I was going to play. I started working with them in 1990 and now in 1991 they were going to play Orion's Belt, and these kids nailed it! This song was high school level. I had a forty-eight piece concert band and my eighth graders were astounding! They were magically good and set the bar high for the others to reach. Call it healthy competition, they brought the rest of the kids up. I was demanding of them and they liked it. They had structure and discipline.

The school was shut down. Thankfully, I was able to pick my next teaching assignment and ended up choosing Blow Middle School in 1993. I was offered to teach percussion at Visual and Performing Arts High School. A woman named Haroldson was going to be laid off, so I chose to stay at Blow Middle and let her keep her job. They gave her the job title of vocal music teacher, unrelated to band, but she got the job as percussion teacher. She didn't know beans about teaching percussion, so I took the after-school position teaching honors music. That was the year I began working six jobs per week. From 7:00 a.m. to 2:00 p.m. I taught band at Blow Middle, on Monday, Wednesday, and Thursday from 3:00 p.m. to 4:30 p.m. and taught the honors music program at Central High School. On Tuesdays, I taught the St. Luke's Catholic School band with fifty-six kids and then I taught privately at my house. I also taught at Fazio Frets and Friends music store on Saturdays and then played in a band on Fridays, Saturdays, and Sundays.

None of the kids knew I was blind. None of them knew something was wrong. They couldn't figure it out. I was a good actor and moved around so well that no one had any suspicions. I learned my environment. Fran would take me into the building and show me where everything was, the entire layout; the bathroom, the counselors' and principals' offices and all the buildings one at a time. Then she would leave. I also had a photographic memory.

Transforming these kids into disciplined, sharp players is a lot of hard work but it pays off. Other public schools would not take part because one, yes, it is a lot of challenging work and nobody had a good band like ours. We did all kinds of parades as well. The May Day and MLK Day parades were two of them. I hated to go because it was in

North St. Louis and I always got in trouble at the end. But we had no choice, so we went. At the time, we marched through the neighborhoods and the crowds would be in the street squeezing the lines. On wider streets you can spread the band out from left to right. The neighborhood streets had us touching each other's elbows and some of them would try to grab the girls. To help keep the riffraff out of the band I marched along with them. The sun would shine on the back of their overlays which was white. The uniforms were dark blue with a white overlay on the back and that helped me follow.

The teaching experiences and notable opportunities I've been able to enjoy are innumerable. I was not a seasoned teacher in the beginning and was thrust into teaching without a clue. Nonetheless, each opportunity was a blessing and ended up being successful, and for that I am grateful and proud. During my four years at Beaumont, I taught a summer program called SLATE at the park near Sumner High School. We formed the Beaumont Sumner Roosevelt Honors Band and had the distinct privilege of performing at the Shriners Auditorium.

In September 1993, I started teaching at Blow Middle School. There was a major gang population attending and no appropriate space to put them. There were seven different gangs at the school. We had Asian kids, we had white and black hoodlums and Aryan Brothers. We had gangs with no room to keep them. There was extra space in the band room with an outside entrance and huge risers that were folded up in front of the doors. Different teachers would come down and watch the class when they were free. The gang-affiliated students had to be monitored otherwise I'm sure they would have taken my life.

So, where does administration decide to place them? The band room, the only extra room on campus. The noise my students made musically drove them nuts, so a teacher was sent down every day to babysit them. They fought so much the room seemed more like detention. Instead of suspending these kids, they were kept in that room. It is understood that these students were kept for financial purposes, but it also served as a torture system. Imagine being on the listening end of kids learning how to play instruments. My kids were not yet virtuosos and their immature playing was undesirable to the ears. Imagine a neighboring room full of gang members having to sit for hours listening to noisy sounding instruments. Their complaints were endless. I had to watch them sometimes while teachers were shifting classrooms. So, I told them, "You know, if you hate this so much, behave in school and you won't have to stay down here." It worked! Those kids got it together just to keep from having to sit downstairs with me and my band students. I found it quite interesting.

CHAPTER NINE

ABLE

When I was laid off in 1983, I began the Able Program. Though I had already learned about cane travel; I did not use it much. At the time the class was reading a book about facial vision. Few blind people have facial vision. So, I listened to what the teacher had to say about it. I thought, "Wow, I believe I have what he's talking about!" They were reading a book and discussing the content with each other. I told my Mobility person I wanted to go for a walk because I wanted to test it out. She was always trying to make sure I knew where I was going.

It was pouring down rain that day and I made sure to bring something to cover my eyes and ears. I put cotton in my ears, pulled the flaps from my cap down over them and put the blindfold on.

We started our walking adventure to test out facial vision. We began to walk up this hill and I could feel eight out of ten trees and all the lamp posts, but there were three objects I missed. The fire hydrant and the street sign because the pole itself was only an inch wide. The third was a mailbox that was lower than my shoulders.

Cane Travel vs. Facial Travel

When I lecture at Washington University I say, "When you close your eyes you can't see anything so you rely on the four senses you have left and then a sixth sense would begin operating." I could sense anything that was close to me. Anything I came close to I felt between my ear and cheekbone. My face would literally warm up. That is facial vision. Not every blind person has this ability. It truly is a gift.

The ABLE program provided apartments for us to live in. Everyone who lived in this building was blind. The girl that lived next door to me was blind and dumb. I was supposed to be living there but only stayed every now and then, more like one night a week or only when I needed to. The program didn't know what I was doing. If I heard staff from the program was coming to the building to check on us, I made certain to be there. At ten or eleven at night I would call Fran to pick me up. To be part of the ABLE program you had to live in the apartments. I really did not want or need one. When I told them, I did not need it they said, "Yeah you do." ABLE believed my having an apartment would help me learn how to live as a blind person. They were dedicated to aiding blind people and held fast to their theory that we needed to learn how to live on their own. I really did not have anyone to talk to and recall staying for a week once and brought my drums with me. I drove everyone nuts with my playing. Hey, I had to practice. So, I did what I had to do then I quickly removed them. I had it down to a science. I would stay at the ABLE apartment for a while, go back to the house and teach, then run back to the apartment and sleep overnight there, and call Fran the next morning to pick me up and take me to ABLE. She would meet me on the corner where I couldn't be seen.

I didn't learn Braille before I went to ABLE. I didn't appreciate having to because learning it, in my mind, meant I was really blind and had to accept it as fact. So, I learned it quickly and moved on to other more interesting subjects. Cooking was fun I have to say. I had a cooking partner who was about five years older than me and totally blind. She made things interesting, educational and fun, and was a worse cook than I. She burned food but did teach me a few things like how to make a dump cake. So, I learned how to cook certain meals and could serve people food that would not make them sick. The only thing I hated about it was having to read recipes in braille. I never surrendered!

I haven't touched braille since leaving school. They even bought me a braille typer that I only typed one letter on. After that, it stayed in my closet for ten years until I finally called a friend to let them know I had one. They offered to take it off my hands. I had the mindset of a sighted person and rejected being blind. Up until 1999, my unwavering way of thinking was "I am not blind."

CHAPTER TEN

THE KIDS FOUND OUT

I taught at Blow Middle School from 1993-1998 and believe the principal, Jim Thompson, ratted me out. I was moved from my usual teaching area because the rooms downstairs had flooded from the rains. When I returned to the classroom two weeks later, my students had adopted new personas and began to try me. At that moment I knew the inevitable would happen quickly. I began packing my things. My stereo, any instruments that were on my desk and all the books. I put everything in my desk and locked it and stowed my briefcase in the instrument room. Once everything was put away, I quietly sat in my chair and waited. The kids went wild. They were jumping all over the place and kicking music stands over. They ran up to where I was sitting and spit on me. They yelled out, "We know you don't know who spit on you!" They ran behind me to try and pull the chair from under me. It was pure hell. I brandished a pair of large marching sticks from my drawer as the bell was about to ring for lunch. I had the girls line up on one side, the boys on the other and I stood in the middle between the lines. Some of them tried to run out of the door, but I wielded my sticks and hit my leg hard causing the kids to jump and back off. One boy asked, "Are you going to hit me with those?" I said, "Yeah!" With one minute left before the lunch bell rang the boys were yelling and refused to be quiet while the girls screamed at them to shut up. I said, "You aren't going anywhere until you get in line and pipe down." It took them three minutes to calm down and stop talking. I finally pushed the left door open, backed up and stood where the door would not hit anyone. They all ran past me and upstairs to the cafeteria because they were late for lunch. There were five hundred twenty-five kids in the entire school and the sixth-grade classes combined totaled one hundred or more. If you were at the end of the cafeteria line, all you would get is what was left over. I sat in my room and thought about the next strategic move I would make when they returned from lunch. The bell rang and they all came back to the room only to find I had locked both doors. They could not enter the room and were knocking to come in. When they asked me to let them in, I just shook my head no and told them they were not coming inside my classroom. They began running through the school hallways screaming and hollering which made the principal furious. He rallied the students together and brought them back. You could hear a pin drop. The principal unlocked my door, walked in and said, "I have your class here," I replied, "I'm not taking them." "What did I say?" he blurted out at me. I said, "No sir, I said they're not allowed to come back in my room!" He repeated his last question, "What did I say?" I then laid it all out, "I called up to the office, talked to the assistant principal, and told her it was an emergency. I told her the kids were rioting and that I was going to get hurt. She did not send anyone, so I sent a girl to find the campus police officer. He also refused to come down. When the officer ignored my call, I knew I was sunk and had to refer to my preservation skills. That meant locking them out of the room until they behaved or left. I made them get in line and walk up the steps to the cafeteria for lunch. From that point on, they were on their own." The principal and I argued for five minutes. I continued saying, "You're telling me that I will take the class and I'm saying, no, I'm not letting these kids in here." He said, "This is your class." I said, "Not anymore!" Again, he repeated with a threatening tone, "This is your class, I'm bringing them in now and I want to see you in my office!" I countered, "Yeah?" He chimed, "Yes!" He warned the kids that if any one of them misbehaved they were going to have to deal with him. He was vein-popping mad, and they knew it. He continued his outburst, "You sit down and don't get up till this bell rings or he tells you what to do." The bell rings and they stumble in line. I let him out the door as quickly as possible. I was supposed to go upstairs at once but I waited five minutes because admittedly, I was a bit stubborn and hard-headed. I entered the administrative office, and his secretary greets me, "Hey Mr. G. what's going on?" I said, "Oh, I just came up." The principal orders me, "Get in here!" I smugly replied, "Did you hear something?" He said, "Mr. Guzman you need to get in here immediately." I said, "Okay." So, I come in and as I'm closing the door, he pulls out a slip of paper to write me up as insubordinate. As he pulls out his paper, I politely asked him to hand me the phone. Puzzled, he asked , "What?" I said, "Yes, can I please use your phone?" He asks, "For what?" I said, "Can I please use your phone?" I did not answer the question and had no idea who I was going to call. He stops and asks me to explain what happened. I said, "Well, I could see there was going to be a mutiny so I packed everything up so nothing would be destroyed and sat in my chair. The kids spit on me and tried to pull the chair out from underneath me. They ran around and brushed against my shoulders and chair. So, I packed everything up. It was all horrendous! I followed procedure and talked to the assistant principal who hates my guts. I asked you to come down and you refused, so I sent the girl to summons the guard and he refused to come down because he was at lunch! I knew I was in serious trouble and would've been physically hurt." The vice principal did not care. She and I had a run-in the year before about my budget.

After this nightmare incident, I knew my teaching days had come to an end. This event was like déjà vu. The year before every seventh and eighth grade kid that came through my class tested me. We were in the back of the school rehearsing the drumline for an upcoming parade. A kid was on the second-floor hollering, and I was below him standing on concrete. I look up and the kid goes, "Oh, you don't know who I am." I turned and said, "When I learn your name, you're in trouble. If you are in my class, I do not have to see you. All you have to do is talk or curse to be in trouble with me." That is what I would tell my sixth graders as new students. "Once I learn your name, you're in trouble because I'll recognize your voice anywhere." The kid standing upstairs was astonished when I said, "Walter, what are you doing up there?" He was shocked and completely floored.

I ran a very tight and good class. The kids learned a lot and enjoyed learning. I was unique and they never had anyone like me.

I had been packing things up little by little. The Friday before, I had two hours free which I used to put my things in the van and the rest store away knowing on Monday I was done.

Monday morning arrived. I went straight to the principal's office and the secretary asked, "Mr. G, what are you doing here? You called in sick." I said, "Yeah, I know I'll be with you in a minute." I asked her if Mr. Thompson was in. He heard me and invited me into his office. Right away I enter his office and hand him my resignation letter. He responded with two words, "I agree." The letter said I was having nervous problems in teaching and I was going out on sick leave. Instead of him saying good-bye, it was nice working with you, he said, "You did things you had to do, and I had to do what I had to do." I reached my hand out over his desk to shake his hand and said, "It was nice working with you, Mr. Thompson." He was a little taken aback. After shaking hands I start to exit, but not without turning around to look him straight in the eyes and say, "Checkmate." Satisfied with the last word, I walked out but I wasn't done. Wanting to redeem my behavior with the eighth grade classes I went to their classrooms and apologized. Lastly, I went to my fellow teachers and informed them of the abuse I had endured at Mr. Thompson's hand. I told them how he would come into my room two or three times a week to condescend me. He would say things like, "I thought I told you to keep your doors unlocked." Every single time I'd apologize and say, "Oh, I'm sorry I forgot. It's just a habit." I handed him a different excuse every time he visited my room. You see, across the hall from my classroom were the emotionally disturbed kids. Next door were the behaviorally disordered kids. All of us were in the school basement. Leaving a door unlocked was a safety issue for students and he knew that. The band room was the size of a basketball room. If I left my band room open, kids would walk in. So, I sat in the middle of the room. The windows were six feet high, so ventilation was poor. It didn't bother me. A little perspiration did not hurt. If someone walked in the room with the door left open, I would not see them or their shadow. My main goal was to guard the instruments and keep myself safe.

I went to the eighth grade teachers and told them what happened. Eighteen teachers and I transferred or retired that summer. There were thirty-three teachers total. To those thirty-three, the principal's behavior with me was unacceptable. He didn't like me because of a statement I made. One day I said, "You were only a typewriting teacher and you're a principal now?" That was the last straw. When school started, he made a teacher transfer because she was handicapped with special needs. After she left, he made the statement that he did not want any handicapped teachers in the building. He put me in a predicament where I had to call the superintendent of music teachers in. He told the superintendent, "I'm the principal here and I can do what I want, and I am doing what I want. These are the real rules he is going to follow." They were arguing about me. That is how much he liked me. I wish I could have seen his face when I said Checkmate. He had to go four months without a music teacher.

The way things ended was unfortunate. The narrative could have ended with integrity and respect. I am blind and that's the truth, but the principal choosing to tell the kids without letting me know first was wrong and deceitful. I retired because my vision had begun to betray me. Concealing it was near impossible. It was too hard to walk around and see everything that was going on around me. If I am honest, I really had not been able to see for the last five years. In

1998, I was in a parade and was left alone in the middle of the street. The light outside was so bright I could not see a thing. The band and everybody took off running and I was left standing there not knowing where the sidewalk was. I begin to walk down the middle of the street and about twenty steps ahead I find one of my kids having an asthma attack. I helped him up, carried his drum and was able to walk with him. Fifteen minutes later we caught up with the band under a tree and finished playing there. At that moment, I knew it was time to go but chose to finish out the year.

In 1999 I retired, but in 2014 I came back to Dubourg as a percussion teacher and taught free of charge. I just wanted to do it and the school is only ten blocks from my house. It was easy for Fran to drive me there and back, and the class only lasted an hour. That summer I was looking forward to teaching a drum clinic. Premiere Drums, Drum Headquarters Drum Store and Fred Pierce Drum Store were sponsoring me as the Clinician. Ten days before the clinic I had a stroke straight down the middle of my body. My playing and speech were the only things affected. Not wanting to let anyone down I worked so hard to be ready physically to teach. When the day came I sat down on my stool to play, but broke down and cried for a moment. After pulling myself together I apologized to the audience. There was no way I was going allow the stroke to make me cancel the event. So, I asked my brother Gene and my son Chuck to stand in for me. It worked out beautifully. The experience was very enjoyable. One hundred twenty-five people showed up and we gave away nine free passes, so the final total was one hundred thirty-four! My boss could not believe it because he was sure only a handful would attend. How do you think I felt telling him the place was packed? It felt great to say the least. The owner let me teach at his store for free all year!

CHAPTER ELEVEN

My Life in Summary

I wasn't looking to be a teacher when I first started college. I was searching for a way to make a decent income. At the time, I was confused about what I could do. Knowing you are going blind brings up all kinds of anxieties and fears. As tough and hardcore as I was on the exterior, my soul on the inside was uneasy and restless. To be perfectly honest, I was compensating for what I lacked emotionally with fierce and sometimes brutal physical strength.

Yes, my early years were a mess. I was a young boy left to raise myself without an instruction manual. I had no visible support from my family and basically had to make it up day by day.

But was I alone? As I stood on top of a new hill, surveying the view from a heightened position, I saw that every struggle, every seeming setback, the intense fighting, and incumbrance of my eye condition, had led me right to where I am purposed to be. I am grateful my life was spared a few times when a proverbial bullet was aimed and purposed to take me out. I believe in a divine power and for me it is God. He positioned me toward a future I am proud to have attained.

One of my most personal and rewarding teaching experiences was the opportunity to teach young people who came from challenging and difficult circumstances. When I say difficult, I mean extremely poor or very abusive environments.

Sheree Moody was one of those young people who has adopted my family as hers. She was playing in one of the school bands at eleven years old. One morning she came to school and was screaming her head off. She was so upset, talking, crying, and screaming at the same time. It was impossible to understand her. When she was finally able to calm down a little, she told me she had been physically abused by her mother. Sheree's mother was a drug addict and an alcoholic. She had walked over to her mother while she was ironing to ask a question. After hearing her story, I took her to a female teacher who examined her and found she had belt buckle marks on her back. The mother was reported, and Sheree was removed from the home immediately. She could go home for Christmas. When she returned to school, her right foot was bandaged. When I asked her what happened she explained, "My mom accidentally fell and cut my foot with her glass." I was beyond angry and screamed at Sheree for making such a stupid mistake. When she returned to her provisional home, I let her take the French horn to practice until she was unfortunately reassigned to a place outside of the city that had the appearance of a jail. I was not going to allow her to feel abandoned and alone so as soon as Fran and I could, we drove to her facility and brought her another French horn to help preoccupy her time. It was not long before she was transferred to another school because of all the fighting and chaos within the system. Sheree was placed in a home for girls in her eighth grade year. About one week later, I got a call that she had run away. She called me and I told her to wait for me. I took my daughter, Sharon with me because I did not want Sheree to detect that I could not see.

The first thing we did was get her some food because she was starving. I hated to tell her that we had to take her back to the home. We kept her out for a little while before returning her. Sheree decided to hang in there and stay at the home for the remaining year. Again, I let her borrow another French horn. After graduating eighth grade, she was sent down near the Ozarks. During the summer between the eighth and ninth grades, she had a fight with a boy over a pack of cigarettes that belonged to her. She ran into the kitchen, grabbed a knife, and told him, "If you come at me, I'm going to stab you!" Either he did not believe her or he did not care because he ran straight to her and she stabbed him, almost killing him. She returned to St. Louis and was locked up again. Troubled kids' pain resonates with me. I know what it is like to be treated with disdain, to be hated and reviled. I could not bring myself to leave this child in jail without support. When Fran and I arrived at the facility, a guard announced who we were coming to visit. I was carrying a guitar and the French horn I had loaned her. This facility was dangerous, and Sheree was the only normal girl there. Everyone else was in for murder or drugs. I gave her the guitar and the French horn and overheard some of the other girls saying, "What are you going to do with that?" She had already been playing for three years and developed into an incredibly good musician. After spending two years in that facility, she was sent to a Foster home in North St. Louis.

At eighteen years old, Sheree attended Riverview Gardens high school. Her foster parents had dropped her like a hot potato and were going to throw her out. They agreed to keep her until she graduated. In the meantime, senior year has a lot of activities that come up like prom, graduation and buying the class ring. She did not have any money for those things and the staff at Riverview were not going to help, so she called me again. Fran and I set up an angel fund account for her. Through this fund and with help from added agencies she was able to raise $18,000 and secure two scholarships. The challenge came when she had to take entrance exams for college. Her ACT score was too low, and she had to take remedial reading and math subjects. Common for Foster children, Sheree did not have a strong educational background as she was often shifted from place to place every six months. I was able to talk St. Anne's music department into giving her a brand new $11,000 double French horn for $5,000. She also had enough money left to buy two great mouthpieces. With all that good fortune she still had no place to live. She even slept on my front porch one night and, for the life of her, couldn't comprehend why she wasn't able to stay inside my house. I really did want to take her in, but as a teacher I would be arrested and fired.

Sheree found places to stay here and there and checked in with us every few days. That summer she continued to take French horn lessons from me. I gave her money for bus fare and food. One day in August, she came by the house while we were barbecuing out back to surprise us with some great news. She announced she'd be attending Warrensburg College in Missouri and was literally leaving right then. I was so happy and proud to congratulate her for making it! She has told us since then that she probably would not be alive today had we not stepped in to help her through her tumultuous seasons. She needed a ride to the train station. So, Fran wrapped up two pieces of corn on the cob for her to take on the train. Sheree remains a part of our lives to this day and I am extremely proud of her.

In 1976, twelve year-old Mike Edsel became one of my private students. He was part of a band at Oak Hill Elementary School playing in the drum and bugle Corps, a group I had started. Like many students, Mike did not grow up with a father in the home and I took him under my wing as a father figure. Before turning seventeen, he would come by the house to take his drum lessons and visit. He always found his way to the kitchen. Not for food to eat, but to lay down on our kitchen floor because he suffered a back injury that caused him severe pain.

He stopped taking lessons when he turned seventeen but continued to stay in touch. During this period, he got a girl pregnant and married her. He had to quit high school but went back to earn his GED. Unfortunately, his wife became a drug user and, with two children, things became increasingly challenging. We tried to help him as best we could. When he turned twenty-three, he needed a financial loan and asked if he could sell me his congas. The deal was, if I ever wanted to sell them, I could sell them right back to him. So, I bought his congas for one hundred fifteen dollars.

Mike went through a very difficult season and sadly his marriage ended in divorce. He continued to study with me on and off and eventually became a teacher himself. He is now fifty-seven years old, still teaches and manages to keep in touch with me by reaching out every holiday.

Bryant Casanover attended Melanphy Middle School. He was eleven years old when he started lessons with me. He was in sixth grade with Donnell Robinson, who I deemed my protégé.

Every day, I donated my lunch time to help kids who needed or wanted extra practice. Bryant Casanover faithfully attended this practice time. His fellow students were mean and told him he sucked, was terrible and even encouraged him to quit. I told them to leave him alone and dug in even harder to help him gain confidence. It was hard for Bryant to find his coordination with the drums and after six months of trying hard, he decided to take private drum lessons. It took him one year to get the first rock beat down. When he turned thirteen, I was teaching a band with a super percussion section. I readied them to perform a piece called "This Old Man" at Central Visual and Performing Arts School. We were given a strict fifteen minutes to get our equipment on stage and perform two pieces. We had to move three drum sets because a piece I wrote called "Suite for Three Drum Sets" required three drums sets. We had to set up the drums, xylophone, a set of bells, a snare drum, a bass drum and four Roto Toms plus move all that equipment off the stage in fifteen minutes. Luckily, we had a few roadies to help us. We managed to get it all done in thirteen and a half minutes and on top of that, received a perfect score by three judges! Bryant was a part of that exciting event. He also got his girlfriend pregnant at the age of seventeen and he too embraced the path of responsibility by asking her to marry him. Bryant also adds to the statistics of growing up without a father in the home. I became his father figure. He ended up becoming quite prosperous in his life. He took a job at Jiffy Lube and every month got a quarter raise because he studied the book and passed the test. When Bryant turned twenty-three, he developed cancer from working with oil and was given one month to live. He brought his beautiful drum set to my house and asked me to sell it after he died so his wife would have money. I kept the set in my basement and refused to sell it, and told him I wouldn't. He had such a hard time accepting his life sentence, so I talked him into going to a doctor I knew at St. Mary's Hospital who oversaw the oncology unit. Bryant is still alive today. The first doctor had given up on him. He is one of my on-again off-again students who comes around every five years or so to take a refresher course. Today Bryant is a successful musician, was partner for a popular sandwich shop called Bellacino's, and now owns his own roofing company. He was successful at every business he worked and told me my work ethics rubbed off on him.

I currently have one young man named JT studying with me that I plan to take to Nashville next summer after he turns sixteen. JT and his family attended Saint Gabriel's church every Sunday night. As I'd be packing my equipment after service, JT would come over and tap on the drums. He was four years old at the time. I gave him a stick and told him to go ahead and try playing with them. That's how it all got started. I gave him his first pair of drumsticks. His mom was a little hesitant at first, but decided not to say anything to discourage him. A practice pad was set up for him at home and I told him the only thing he could hit was the pad, not his sister or anything else. My sisters used to take my sticks and hit me with them. JT listened. He was a good kid. When he was seven years old, he started drum lessons and has been with me ever since. He is fifteen years old now and plays like he is twenty-five. I recently gave him my collection of books, "Fifty-Nine Trombones," a series written by Joe Rothman. His mother and father work in the medical field. Because of the current situation with the coronavirus, his parents will not allow him to take lessons in person so we meet over the telephone. He plays the xylophone at college level JT is gifted and, in fact, plays "Flight of the Bumblebee" at full tempo with a metronome.

After I played the first couple of songs during service, I would have him come up and take my place. I'd hand him the drums sticks and let him take over for the rest of the mass. I would sit behind him and whisper instructions because he was trying to learn balance. It was a good teaching aspect for him. For the last ten summers my band has played at Children's Hospital, the same hospital where his parents work. We call JT to come and sit in with us and, boy, he loves it. He is still in high school. Sometime last year his band director told him that when he reaches his junior year, he will be the best musician in one of the top schools in the city, St. Louis University High School.

When teaching, my goal was to reach out to as many kids and students as possible and give them a music education that was be hard to beat. That's why I always undercharged in comparison to the music stores. I wanted kids to be able to take music classes and not stand on the outside wishing, hoping, and praying that they could one day do the same. I could provide that service with a minimal charge. This was my way of helping them. For an hour or so a day, they could escape into the world of music, learn a skill that could either provide a future income or help them grow. One excellent way of enhancing quality of life is through music. It is also a positive distraction from drug/alcohol use and gang involvement. Some children's lives were saved and that stands at the top of my list of things I am most grateful for. Laval, Sheree, Bryant, Mike and JT are a handful of young people I have been able to influence. Did they all become great successes? Some did, and they all walked away from me feeling someone authentically cared and desired nothing more than their good fortune. That was very important to me.

There was a time during 1997-1998 that I contemplated quitting teaching. I frantically worked what I thought would be my last crop of students into playing great that year because I knew my teaching days were coming to an end. During this time, I involved the band in several parades and concerts. Our last concert was held at 6:00 in the evening on the front lawn of Blow Middle in 1998. It was a huge success with three to four hundred people in attendance.

To my surprise, at the end of the 1998 school year, I was awarded Teacher of the Year by my colleagues. You never know how others see and value you. Their generosity gave me the second wind I needed to continue touching the lives of young people through music and encouragement.

Teaching was a gift God granted to me. I believe we have all been given one or even many gifts for that matter, but there are other rudimentary principles in life that add fulfillment. Being able to accomplish tasks that add harmony to the home is important to me. I was determined to help with day to day chores around the house. Being blind did not exempt me from doing my part to the best of my ability. I never used my lack of eyesight as a crutch. Never! Humbly speaking, I can do some things better than those blessed with 20/20 vision!

For the last thirty years I've been hanging Christmas lights on the exterior of my house. My grandkids were my inspiration to begin this winter ritual. I'm talking to my wife's chagrin I charge full steam ahead to make my grandkids happy and myself creatively satisfied.

On December 24, 2018, at 4:55 p.m. the entertainment television news outlet, Inside Edition visited to interview and record me standing on my ladder installing lights on the back side of the house. The title of the show is called Southside Blindman.

From time to time, the neighbors and some of my friends come by and yell for me to "Get down off of that ladder, you're crazy!" Forgetting that I'm blind they continue with, "It's dark outside and you're hanging lights!" I find it so amusing! Believe it or not, I haven't experienced one accident and can proudly say the lights are as straight as can be!

Not only do I hang lights, I've added a twenty-five foot Santa Claus to the rooftop chimney, a manger scene with Jesus, Mary and Joseph

on the front lawn, a lighthouse and two large candles. There's icicle lights hanging, stars with rays shooting downward, lights around the windows with one window dedicated to my granddaughter Abby. Little bitty star lights are placed to make it appear as though one is looking up at the galaxy. Every year I add new lights to my winter wonderland. The entire project takes two weeks to complete and I enjoy every minute! I have a full life, beyond what I could have asked for. I'm a man with a visual impairment who decided not to use my condition as a crutch. My choice to do so made room for me to stretch out and play in a few bands. I still play in a band that I've been a part of since 1995 called Presentations. This group of talented musicians still challenge and inspire me today. The first two years we played together I booked us one hundred ninety-five gigs per year, and we were paid a hundred dollars a night. That was twenty-four years ago. In 1997, we played in the Ozarks at SIU and all kinds of interesting places. Unfortunately, bands are not hirable at present because of COVID-19, but as soon as the quarantine lifts we look forward to getting back out there.

I've taught at eight middle and high schools, eight music stores, taught my own private lessons from 1974 to present and played with top quality musicians and bands, as a blind man!

I am humbled at the many opportunities I have been given. I do not take my blessings for granted. The capacity to play twenty-one instruments, the privilege of teaching every student I've encountered, being able to play for the church over the years are things I hold in the highest regard and will never take for granted. Equipping students with skills that can carry them to places they never imaged and sustain their lives fills me with the greatest joy. I wouldn't trade my path in life for anything in this world, the negative or the sweet. For it has led me to the greenest of pastures and brought wealth to my soul that can't be measured in gold.

I have the best wife and children one could ask for and a special little addition that came to us later in life, my beautiful Abby, my granddaughter who I helped raise.

I hope my life and story will be used to influence and transform not only those without sight, but anyone who has obstacles in their lives that make them believe they can't achieve success. If I can make it, you can too!

CHAPTER TWELVE
An Ode to Rich

I met Rich in 1981 when I opened Drum Headquarters, a music store that sold percussion items only and offered lessons. He taught at Drum Headquarters from about 1982-87.

His ability to navigate throughout a retail store that was chock-full of merchandise was incredible. He knew the location of his teaching studio, the bathroom, the front counter and where different merchandise was displayed throughout the shop.

Rich's memory was astounding. He had numerous drum instruction books memorized, so he could direct a student to play a certain passage by page and exercise number. Since he knew the books backwards and forwards, he could tell from memory when a student didn't play something correctly.

Rich endeared himself to his students. The students knew he cared about them and he made the lessons fun, even though he had a reputation as a taskmaster about the basics. He was fiercely loyal to them and it was returned to him ten-fold. Because of this, his students stayed with him longer than the average.

~*Rob Birenbaum*

For Speaking Engagements, Book Signings,
Appearances, and Interviews...

Contact

Richard J. Guzman
314-352-3950
guzmanmusic@hotmail.com